Landmark

Tenerife

Brian & Eileen Anderson

WITH COMPLIMENTS
from
PRESTIGE HOLIDAYS
Tel: 01425 480400

Published by
Landmark Publishing
Ashbourne Hall, Cokayne Ave, Ashbourne,
Derbyshire DE6 1EJ England

Contents

Welcome To Tenerife   6

Location and Landform	9
Arts and Culture	12
Food and Drink	12
Climate	16
When To Go	17
Where To Stay	20
Natural Environment	20
History	21

1. Touring and Exploring   30

Resort Guide	31
El Médano	31
Costa del Silencio	32
Los Cristianos	32
Playa de las Américas	32
Playa Paraiso	32
Puerto de Santiago	33
Los Gigantes	33
Puerto de la Cruz	33
Good Beach Guide	33
Playa De Las Teresitas	35
El Médano	36
Los Cristianos	36
Playa de las Américas	37
Puerto Santiago	37
San Marcos	37
Los Realejos	37
Puerto de la Cruz	37

2. Days Out   38

A Day Out in La Gomera	39
A Day Out at Loro Parque	41
A Day Out in Puerto de la Cruz	45
A Day Out in Santa Cruz	49

3. Car Tours   54

The Silent South	55
Teide National Park	56
The Orotava Valley	62
The Teno Mountains	65
The Anaga Peninsula	68

Fact File   72

Getting There	72
Accommodation	72
Car Hire	74
Motorcycles	75
Changing Money	75
Complaints	75
Consulates	76
Crime and Theft	76
Currency and Credit Cards	77
Disabled Facilities	77
Driving on Tenerife	78
Duty-free Allowances	79
Electricity	79
Emergency Telephone Numbers	79
Health Care	80
International Dialling Codes	81
Lost Property	81
Mosquitoes	81
Museums	81
National Tourist Office	81
Nightlife	82

Nudism	83	Markets	86
Police	83	Sports and Pastimes	88
Postal Services	83	Telephone Services & Internet	92
Public Holidays and Festivals	84	Tenerife Time	92
Public Toilets	85	Tipping	92
Public Transport	85	Tourist Offices	92
Shopping	86	Water	93

Feature Boxes

Top Tips 7
Whale Watching 17
Flowers of Tenerife 22
Travel Tips 27
Beach Safety 33
Bananera el Guanche 44
Family Entertainment in the South 40
Family Entertainment in the North 47
Carnival 50
Walking Hell's Valley (Barranco del Infierno) 57
The Pyramids of Güímar 61

Welcome to
Tenerife

Opposite page: Nuestra Señora de la Peña de Francia, Puerto de la Cruz

Myth and mystery has shrouded the Canary Islands from birth. Fiery flames, towering plumes of ash and huge lava flows marked their arrival millions of years ago during a period of intense volcanic activity and their location can only be described as fortunate.

Top Tips

1. Pico de Teide and Las Cañadas
The cable car to the peak only operates when the snow declines and the wind permits but the weird and wonderful landscapes of Las Cañadas are there to enjoy at all times.

2. Anaga peninsula
Dramatic landscapes of mountains and rocky coastlines.

3. La Orotava
An atmospheric old town with traditional architecture and museums including the famous House of Balconies (Casa de los Balcones).

4. Masca
A tiny village in an awesome location perched out on a ridge.

5. Santa Cruz
Museums, interesting architecture and good shopping.

6. Puerto de la Cruz
The most interesting and attractive resort on the island, good shopping.

7. Loro Parque (Puerto de la Cruz)
Brilliant display of exotic birds and mammals, shows with sea lions, dolphins and parrots: a great family day out.

8. Siam Park (Adeje)
A new aquatic theme park with a myriad attractions, including a man-made beach and wavepool.

9. Neighbouring La Gomera
A beautiful unspoilt island within easy sailing distance.

10. The amazing pyramids at Güímar (p61)

Pitched in the Atlantic Ocean off the coast of Africa, the Canaries are blessed with abundant sunshine and great fertility.

Their presence is acknowledged in early legends as the Elysian Fields, the garden of Hesperides, Atlantis or simply the mythical lands beyond Hercules' Column (the Straits of Gibraltar). Despite their modern role in tourism, the element of mystique still lingers. They represent an 'out of Europe' experience offering unique volcanic landscapes testifying to their agonising birth, black beaches and a flora which draws its inspiration from the desert and the tropics.

Tenerife is the largest and most popular of the seven main islands which make up the Canaries. Surprisingly, in view of its popularity, it is not exactly teeming with great beaches (see the Good Beach Guide, p33-37) but it does offer sunshine all year round and a remarkable variety of scenic experiences and places to visit. Mount Teide, reaching an altitude of 3,718m (12,199ft), is an irresistible draw for visitors and its roughly central location means that it can be reached with equal facility from all parts of the island. Otherwise there is perhaps more sightseeing in the lush north than in the arid south, although the island is not so large and most parts can be reached by car within the day. For those happy to hire a car, three or four days will be sufficient to visit most of the major sites on the island. Suggested itineraries are detailed in the Out and About section which follows.

Always drier than the fertile north, the southern part of the island attracted just small settlements throughout the years but all that changed in the 1960s with the advent of mass tourism. The southernmost part of the island had all the ideal ingredients to attract developers, almost continual sunshine and plenty of accessible coastline. Playa de las Américas grew rapidly from nothing to become the largest holiday resort on the island followed by the adjacent Los Cristianos. Today they accommodate a huge proportion of the tourists visiting the island.

In contrast, much of the island's history lies in the north. Here, a touch more rain and cloud has made life easier for the farmers and encouraged the development of larger towns. Santa Cruz, the capital, lies in the north as does La Laguna and Puerto de la Cruz and, although not untouched by tourism, these offer the best places for visitors to enjoy and absorb some Spanish culture.

If the attractions of sun, sightseeing, history and culture are not enough, the accent now has turned to fun. Theme parks are a growth industry: the biggest and best at the moment is Loro Parque at Puerto de la Cruz with its exotic birds and performing sea lions and dolphins but there are aquatic parks, banana plantations, zoos, camel safaris and all sorts of attractions springing up. Sports enthusiasts will not be disappointed either; there is a good choice from walking and golf through to water sports. Tenerife is heading for the complete holiday island. It is all on offer from lively and boisterous to the quiet and peaceful; it just requires a little care in making the right choices before you go.

Location & Landform

Tenerife lies in the middle of the Canary Islands which form a broad line off the coast of North Africa. La Gomera, clearly visible from the west coast of Tenerife, Hierro and La Palma all lie to the west while Gran Canaria, Fuerteventura and Lanzarote arc away to the east.

With an area of 2057sq km (793sq miles), it is the largest island of the group and is also home to Spain's highest mountain, Pico de Teide, reaching up to an altitude of 3,718m (12,199ft). Snow caps the peak for a period in the midwinter months and is usually enough to bring the cable car to a halt for a period. Just below and surrounding this dominant peak is an enormous collapsed crater known as Caldera de las Cañadas. Full of crater rims, solidified lava and fascinating rock formations, this extraordinary moonscape is protected as part of the National Park of Teide. From this relatively flat area the land then falls away irregularly towards the coast. There are two other mountain ranges of note, although both are much lower in altitude. The Anaga mountains lie north-east of Santa Cruz and the Teno mountains in the west. Both areas are particularly scenic and well visited by tourists.

Gorges (*barrancos*) cut deep into the mountains in some parts but few of them carry watercourses. One notable exception is Barranco del Infierno, near Adeje. With its stream and waterfall, this gorge is one of the best known and is particularly popular with walkers. Valleys too are a feature of the lower slopes and two of these in particular, La Orotava and Güimar, provide highly productive growing areas that are fully exploited.

Although the south has some low-lying areas, there are few areas of plain on the island. In general, the mountains decline steadily to meet the sea, often terminating in rugged cliffs relieved by bays and coves, sometimes with beaches of black sand.

The Canary Islands were born of volcanic activity and, in geological terms, are still youngsters. Tenerife and La Gomera were the last to appear some 12 to 8 million years ago. Fortunately, the volcanic activity on Tenerife is relatively subdued these days and there has not been any significant activity since an eruption at Chinyero, just to the north west of Pico de Teide, in 1909.

The whole geology of the island is dominated by dark volcanic rocks and lava flows which have been further sculptured by the weather to produce some weird and wonderful landscapes. This is at its most spectacular at Caldera de las Cañadas, the old crater just below the peak of Teide. If the bluish black basalt seems to dominate, other rock types can be picked out like the greyish-green phonlite, the frothy pumice which is so full of holes that it actually floats on water, grey trachite and glassy obsidian.

With time, weathering of these volcanic rocks produces a good, fertile soil rich in minerals but there are still regions of the island, especially in the south, where this has not yet taken place. The consequence is that some areas look almost totally barren.

Tenerife

Dragon Tree

Welcome to Tenerife

Churros con chocolate

Loro Parque Orca whales

Arts and Culture

There is no evidence now of artistic influences of the indigenous culture; this was supplanted by the settlers from Spain bringing along their own customs and habits. The early churches and public buildings were modest but as they developed they turned to the architectural styles of Europe. Examples of Gothic are not common but the Renaissance style is easy to find. Gradually, the architecture started to show individuality, especially in the ornamentation. Woodcarving became a feature and made its appearance in finely carved wooden ceilings made from Canarian pine and in carved wooden balconies which are still a feature of the island's architecture. The House of the Balconies in La Orotava is the place to see some exquisitely carved old wooden balconies.

Music and customs slowly diverged from the original Spanish and over the centuries the islanders discovered their own folk songs which are still sung on the island today. The islanders love their music and Tenerife boasts a highly regarded symphony orchestra which is active in presenting concerts of classical music around the island while La Laguna has its own classical orchestra.

One of the enduring traditions is that of the fiestas. These usually have a religious element which means the occasion opens with a procession from the local church but it soon moves on to pleasures of a more secular nature. The big event of the year is carnival (*carnaval*) which takes place some time around Shrove Tuesday in Santa Cruz and is repeated in Puerto de la Cruz and Los Cristianos in the weeks following. It is a huge and colourful event and a great draw for visitors. More information is given on P50.

Food and Drink

The quality of meals all around the island is generally good. Beef, usually from South America with whom Tenerife has close ties, pork, lamb, chicken, turkey, rabbit and fish are all freely available and feature on most menus.

Apart from good Canarian dishes, just about everything is available in Playa de las Américas and Los Cristianos, from fast food to fish and chips. Roast beef dinners on a Sunday are often the order of the day and English breakfast is offered just about everywhere, often at a very competitive price. Other cuisines are well represented and it is possible to eat Chinese, Italian, Greek, Indian or even Thai.

Although broadly similar to the Spanish, the islands do have their own distinctive cuisine which developed to meet the need of the peasants and made practical use of readily available ingredients. Perhaps one of the dishes which the visitor is most likely to encounter is Canarian potatoes served with *mojo* sauce. This is often listed amongst the starters and is served in some restaurants as a matter of course while customers are awaiting the first course. Invariably the potatoes are small, cooked in their skins with plenty of salt (*papas arrugadas*) while the *mojo* sauce is served in a separate dish. A red *mojo* sauce is usually hot and spicy so it is wise to try a small sample to make sure it is to taste before proceeding. The red sauces take their colour from the powdered red pepper used in the recipe, which may also include crushed garlic, cumin seeds and oil. Not all *mojo* sauces are spicy; some recipes use coriander in place of the red pepper giving a green sauce and others may even contain cheese.

Gofio, a flour made from a roasted grain, is less important in the islanders' diet now but it is still encountered. The grain may be wheat, barley or maize. It was used in a variety of ways, perhaps with milk at breakfast as part of a cereal or even over fruit such as banana but these days it is mainly used to thicken soups and stews or kneaded to make a kind of bread. This is sometimes served in restaurants in place of bread. One of the meat specialities which is particularly favoured by the islanders is *conejo con salmorejo,* or rabbit *salmorejo* served in a spicy tomato sauce.

Fish (*pescado*) is something of a speciality on the island and an important part of the Canarian diet. To sample the best, head for the fish restaurants in the small fishing villages, like Los Abrigos in the south, which have a fine reputation. Fish is mostly cooked quite simply, either boiled, fried or grilled, but may be served with a spicy sauce and is usually accompanied by boiled potatoes. Some of the fish on offer are unfamiliar, like the delicate, white *vieja*, nor do their names always translate to anything familiar, but others are well known. *Salmón* (red mullet), *sardinas* (sardines), *atún* (tuna), *lenguado* (sole), *cherne* (sea bass family), *pulpo* (octopus), *calamares* (squid, mostly served as deep rings under the name of 'Calamares a la Romana'), *camarones* (shrimps), *mejillones* (mussels) and *lagostinos* (giant prawns) all feature strongly amongst the selection offered by fish restaurants. Paella is enormously popular but is usually only made for two or more people. It does vary considerably; the best ones are usually enjoyed at a fish restaurant while the frozen 'instant' version will probably appeal most to fast food addicts. Another Tenerifian dish to watch out for is *zarzuelos* which is a plate of mixed fish.

Salads are ever present, as a starter or with a meal. In a typical Tenerifian restaurant (*restaurant tipico*), the salads can be quite an adventure and may contain a whole range of interesting ingredients from avocado pears to kiwi fruit to supplement the more usual olives, green peppers, lettuce, tomato and cucumber. They are large too and one, as a starter, is often enough to feed two people.

Desserts are often quite limited and usually include fresh fruit, especially the Canarian banana, flan (rather like crème caramel) or ice cream, although *bienmesabe* might just be on the menu. This is a sweet concoction featuring honey and almonds with perhaps a touch of rum or liqueur.

Drinks

Beer (*cerveza*) is commonly drunk with meals as is spring water which may be carbonated (*con gas*) or still (*sin gas*). Spanish wines are prominent on the wine lists but many of these are indifferent wines at not exactly cheap prices. The Rioja labels, especially for red wine drinkers, are usually the most reliable in quality. Tenerifian wines are also available but, to be sure, check that there is a label showing a map of the

Teide National Park

island indicating the region where it was produced.

The island's wine industry is rising again after years in the doldrums. Vines were introduced by the various settlers, Spanish, Portuguese, French, Flemish, Genoese, from the 16th century onwards, each bringing a selection of their own favourite varieties. Recent years have seen a considerable revival of interest and many of the old varieties are still around. Curiously, the outbreak of phylloxera which totally devastated the vineyards of Europe left Tenerife untouched. The result now is that Tenerife is, in effect, a museum of old varieties grown as they were three centuries ago. Organisation is creeping back into the system and the island is divided into five regions for viniculture depending on the topography and the soil types present.

Climate

Eternal spring is the phrase most commonly used to describe Tenerife's mild climate. Certainly the climate is more equable than would be expected even at those southern latitudes but the prevailing Trade Winds and the cool Canary Currents help to control major fluctuations. As a result of these influences it is rarely especially cold in winter and likewise not too hot in summer. Average January temperatures are around 18.4°C on the coast which rises just a few degrees to 24.8°C in August.

Rainfall, which in a normal year is not particularly high, is confined to the winter months and, as a consequence of the prevailing winds and topography of the island, falls mainly in the north although the difference between north and south in the summer months is negligible. On account of its higher rainfall, the north is lush and green compared to the arid south.

Sun seems almost a perpetual feature, especially in the south of the island. Over the short days of winter, the sun shines on average six hours every day. This is hot, burning sunshine and sunbathers will need to protect their skin with great care. Hours of sunshine increase with day length, reaching a maximum in July and August of around ten hours per day.

Cloud is an important feature, particularly on the western side of the island, which is a further consequence of the Trade Winds. Although the day might start clear, cloud banks form around the mountain at an altitude of around 650m (2,130ft) during the morning. These slowly build out seawards and persist only to clear as the day cools. This phenomenon occurs all year round. The cloud does not usually bring rain but the vegetation in the cloud belt on the mountainside benefits from the mist that condenses on the leaves or drips from the trees above.

Winds are a fairly regular feature. The main culprit is the Trade Winds blowing steadily from the north-east which are responsible for bringing the rain to the north of the island. They are cooling in summer, well loved by the windsurfers but rarely strong enough to cause discomfort. When the south-easterlies blow, it is a different matter. Coming from the Sahara Desert, they are hot and dusty, often depositing Saharan sand and making the atmosphere very hazy.

When To Go

Tenerife, like the rest of the Canary Islands, enjoys sunshine all year round. Since it is the nearest place to Europe which holds out the prospect of hot sunny days in winter, prices of hotels and car hire are just as high in winter as they are in midsummer. Prices dip a little from the end of April until June and in November and December. Peak demand is experienced over Christmas and New Year and this is reflected in the prices, which are usually higher than in August. Car hire prices show little variation between summer and winter.

Winter days offer plenty of opportunity for sunbathing, either on the beach or around the hotel pool, but water sports facilities are not always fully available. Other facilities are much the same winter and summer with theme parks and aquaparks open all year. Walkers certainly enjoy the best conditions in winter when the days are not quite so hot but visitors wishing to use the cable car to visit the summit of Teide are best advised to consider the summer months. Even so, the cablecar does not function in high winds which can occur

Whale Watching

The seas off the south coast of Tenerife are rich in whales, dolphins, water turtles, flying fish and much more. There are organised whale-watching trips out of most harbours around the southern end of the island, from Puerto Colón in Playa de las Américas and from Los Gigantes in particular. Some boats offer a mix of activities. After spending the early part of the trip searching for whales they then return to some secluded bay for swimming and sangria. On the other hand, whale safaris tend to follow the whales for a much longer period.

Pilot whales, which form very large groups of a hundred or more are resident in the channel between La Gomera and Tenerife where they feed on soft animals such as squid but the list of species seen in these parts is considerably larger and includes the killer whale, the fin whale, the minke whale, the goose-beaked whale, the sperm whale right down to the endangered Bryde's whale. Dolphins too are just about as prolific and include the bottlenose dolphin, the common dolphin, the rough-toothed dolphin and Risso's dolphin.

There is an awareness of conservation amongst the serious whale watch fraternity and they are careful not to get too close to the whales and often cut their engines to let the whales swim past undisturbed. Whales surface regularly to breathe and are easily hit, so speeds are kept down when it is known that whales are in the vicinity and there is agreement not to allow too many boats around the same pod of whales.

Tenerife

Tenerife Elephants

Welcome to Tenerife

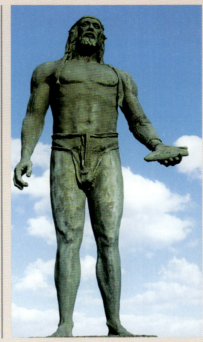

Statues of Guanche Kings Romen and Pelicar at Candelaria

Golf Amarilla

just as frequently in summer.

Summer temperatures are only a few degrees higher and the days are only a little longer but the place has more of a buzz. The number of visitors is swollen by Spanish holidaymakers from the mainland and a younger set are very much in evidence. Nightlife is available all year round but it swings a little more vigorously in summer.

Where To Stay

There is a surprisingly small choice of resorts on the island and these are largely in the southern half. Generally, the north is greener, lusher and more picturesque than the south with a bigger share of old villages and places of interest for sightseers. The south scores with better all-year-round weather. In summer the weather should not deter visitors from choosing freely, north or south, since all areas are dry and largely sunny. In winter the situation is a little different for the south is more reliably sunny and drier than the north.

Natural Environment

The drive from the southern airport through the arid countryside gives visitors an early glimpse of the plant life. Cactus-like candlesticks of *Euphorbia canariensis* cluster around the dry rock. This is one of the many endemic species shared perhaps with other islands in the group, and maybe even Madeira, but seen nowhere else. Euphorbias are well represented on the island, often in these drier zones amongst the prickly pear (*Opuntia ficus indica*),

but looking more like succulent plants or cactus than the European species. Looking more familiar are the shrubby plants covered with white daisies, *Argryranthemum* species, which flower in the early part of the year. Different and often more colourful flowers are found at low levels in the less arid regions. Two familiar British weeds, the sow-thistle and the ragwort, have exotic cousins living on Tenerife. The *Sonchus* species related to the sow-thistle show exuberant growth and carry large clusters of yellow flowers. *Senecio* species, on the other hand, abandon their normal yellow garb for a delightful purple colour. *Echiums* (viper's bugloss family) too are strikingly different from their European cousins and some species grow to truly gigantic proportions. Perhaps the most famous of these is *E. wildprettii* which has a towering spike of red flowers and is found in the subalpine zone below Mount Teide.

The north of the island is more forested. At one time there was an extensive evergreen forest of laurel. The activities of man have reduced this to insignificance but it does hide different flowers such as the *Geranium canariense*, *Convolvulus canariensis* and the Canarian bell, *Canarina canariensis*, although the latter can be found where there are shrubs for it to scramble over. Pine forests, usually at higher levels, are more extensive thanks to reforestation programmes. The native pine, *Pinus canariensis*, a Canarian endemic, has been in great demand over the centuries for its timber.

Oleander, hibiscus, bougainvillaea and poinsettia are amongst the ornamental plants that grow luxuriously on Tenerife and are widely seen in parks and gardens. Poinsettias in particular seem entirely at home and grow into small trees reaching up to 3-4m (10–13ft).They have also found a place in the countryside and their bright red bracts brighten up the northern vegetation in winter. The bird of paradise flower, *Strelitzia*, grows well too and is grown commercially for export and for visitors to take home. Perhaps the most ubiquitous of the decorative trees is the Canary palm, *Phoenix canariensis*, which has a beautiful full crown. It is closely related to the date palms of North Africa but it produces only small dates which are inedible. Tenerife's most famous tree is the dragon tree, *Dracaena draco*, thanks to a particularly old specimen at Icod which has become something of a tourist attraction. Belonging to the Agave family, its many branches intertwine to form a spreading crown reaching up to a height of 20m (65ft).

The fauna is by no means as rich as the flora. Happily for walkers, there are no snakes or scorpions but there are lizards of which the largest is the Canarian lizard growing to around 30cm (12in). There are no large mammals, just rabbits, hedgehogs and bats, unless the wild sheep, mouflons, are included. Mouflons were introduced for the hunters but now just cause problems by eating the wild flowers. Birdwatchers will be a little happier although they might be disappointed by the wild canary which is a brown-backed yellow-chested finch and nothing like as bright as the domesticated species. Amongst the really colourful species to be seen are the hoopoe and the great woodpecker but these apart there is a whole range of familiar birds to capture with binoculars including buzzards, kestrels, blue tits, grey wagtails and, of course, seagulls.

Some of the most exciting fauna lies beneath the waves. The Atlantic around Tenerife is home to a number of whale colonies and various kinds of dolphins.

History

The Guanches

Just how, when and by whom the Canaries were first settled remains an enigma. The early people of Tenerife were called the Guanches, which in old Canarian language means 'sons of Tenerife'. Early settlers on other islands in the group were named differently, usually after their islands, but it is generally believed that they all had similar origins. There is little doubt that they arrived by boat and very probably by reed boat. Denied the reeds to repair or maintain their boats, they became isolated and it seems that there was no further contact between the different islands subsequent to their arrival. Still unanswered is the question of when they actually arrived. It seems that the ancient Guanches had no knowledge of metals, their tools were made of wood and the first cutting weapons of stone. This suggests their break with civilisation took place in the Neolithic period and perhaps they arrived in the Canaries as early as 3,000 BC. Some historians place them rather later, perhaps 1,000 BC.

Flowers of Tenerife

Canarian bellflower

Bougainvillaea

Hibiscus flower

Bird of paradise flower

Poinsettia

Social structure

When the Spanish conquerors arrived in 1494, they found an island divided into nine kingdoms, each governed by a *mencey* (a king). A hierarchical system was in place with, in effect, a deputy king, nobles and peasants. Nobility was not hereditary; it was something to be earned by good works and a

Welcome to Tenerife

Aquapark

Los Silos

community conscience. Laws were in place to keep social order and thieves, for example, were severely punished as decreed by the king in consultation with his counsellors. They had a religion, a belief that there was a single god, Oborac, who was all-powerful. Each tribe had its own priests and places of worship, usually sacred caves. Oborac had an adversary in Guyota who lived in the volcanic crater of Teide and punished the misdeeds of men with volcanic eruptions.

They farmed to survive, both by herding and agriculture. With only the most basic of tools, they managed to grow and harvest grain, including barley and wheat. Housing was quite a different problem. They lived in caves where possible or else in huts, unlike Gran Canaria where they built houses of stone. Tools and utensils were very basic although some handsome pieces of pottery survived through to the Spanish era, but this was made without the use of a wheel.

In common with people from ancient Egypt and Peru, the Guanches embalmed their dead but by a process which was very primitive. The mummies decayed over time but there were still plenty found by the Spanish invaders and some of these are on display in the museum.

Of the language there is scant knowledge since the Spanish invaders found no written documents and all that remains is the place names. Some authorities draw comparisons with the Berber language but the lightweight evidence still leaves it open to debate. It is believed the language was common to all the islands but varied in dialect. Rock drawings and possible script have been found on some islands but not on Tenerife.

The Spanish conquest

The conquest of the Canary Islands started around 1402 with the arrival of the Spanish on Lanzarote. Jean de Béthencourt, a Norman lord backed by Henry III of Castile led the force. It was another 94 years before the Canary Islands were fully under the control of the Spanish. Tenerife did not yield easily. After resisting a number of early attempts, the Guanches were well on their guard. Fernández de Lugo, backed by a force of 1,200 men, landed on the beach near Santa Cruz to find little resistance. His task was made easier by the fact that four of the kingdoms had declared neutrality. He marched first to La Laguna without problems and then onwards to La Orotava where Lugo and his troops rounded up some

livestock before deciding to return. Some 300 Guanches were waiting in ambush at the Barranco de Acentejo, just 16km (10miles) to the east of Puerto de la Cruz, and launched a fierce attack on the unsuspecting Spaniards. The Spanish were massacred and only about a quarter of the Spanish force escaped, including Lugo. Barranco de Acentejo is now called La Matanza (the massacre).

Lugo returned with another force of 700 Spaniards plus some islanders, but this time was more prepared for battle. The Guanches were waiting at La Laguna but many were killed in the battle that followed and they finally withdrew. Lugo returned to Santa Cruz and stayed there several months before setting forth again to what proved to be the final battle. On 25 December 1495, with the advantage of firearms and crossbows, the Spanish overcame the Guanches' resistance. Many were killed while others fled into the mountains.

The Guanches as a people were all but annihilated. Many were killed, some were enslaved and shipped away to the mainland and the rest simply absorbed and assimilated over time. Many claim that Guanche features can be observed in some of the Canarians even today.

The growth of trade

Fernández de Lugo settled on the island, established La Laguna as the capital, set up sugar plantations in the north and died a rich man. Sugar became the first commercial crop and was grown in all the lowland areas and adjoining valleys. In the middle of the 16th century, the sugar trade was thrown into crisis and effectively destroyed by competition from new plantations in America, Brazil and the West Indies. Fortunately, the wine trade was in a growth phase and Malvasia much in demand. Markets were rapidly established in America amongst the new colonists and Europe, bringing a new wealth to the island in the 16th and 17th centuries.

A fierce eruption of Teide in 1706 poured lava down onto Garachico, the main port of that time, completely destroying the town and port. It severely affected the wine trade for a time but it led to the development of other ports, first Puerto de la Cruz and later Santa Cruz, which became capital of the island in 1723.

Lying on busy sea routes to America and the far east brought other problems, namely smuggling and pirates. Spain prohibited slavery but Tenerife was too convenient as a marshalling yard for slaves from Africa prior to their long journey to America so the trade continued as an illegal activity. Pirates added to the lawlessness of this period, attracted to these waters by the Spanish bullion ships using the Canaries as a port of call on their voyages from Mexico. To add to the mischief, English fleets on more than one occasion sailed into Santa Cruz to wreak havoc. It was the turn of Admiral Blake in 1656, who sailed into Santa Cruz and scuttled 16 Spanish galleons carrying gold bullion. The island's fortifications were built in this period.

Nelson's attack

In 1797, Rear-Admiral Horatio Nelson commanding eight warships sailed into Santa Cruz to take the town. Leading 1,000 men, Nelson attempted a landing at midnight on 24 July but the flotilla of small boats was tossed by the rough seas and thrown onto the rocks. Many boats were unable to reach the landing point. They came under heavy fire too from the fortress defended by General Gutiérrez. Except for a few small groups, the English were driven back and Nelson received a wound in his right elbow from a cannon ball which led to the amputation of his arm. The following morning, Spanish troops gathered up the remainder of the English soldiers and sent them back to their ships carrying gifts of food while the wounded were treated in hospital. Peace was signed and gifts and letters of friendship were exchanged between Nelson and Gutiérrez before the English fleet left for home.

Free trade

In the first half of the 19th century the island's economy was not so robust. The wine trade, on which Tenerife depended so heavily, declined after the re-establishment of trade between England, France and Portugal on conclusion of the Peninsular War and the government was forced to look in other directions. With the support of Queen Isabella II, the Canaries were declared a free trade zone in 1852 and, with the advent of the steamship and growing sea trade, the island's economy was once again boosted.

Reviving agriculture

Other measures were still needed so the government introduced fiscal measures

25

Tenerife

Hotel Jardin, Playa de las Américas

Lido Martianez

Welcome to Tenerife

Titsa, local bus service

Travel Tips

1. Tenerife is not an island renowned for its beaches so be sure to choose a hotel with a good swimming pool and sunbathing area. See Good Beach Guide p33-37 for more detail.

2. Take extra special care sunbathing. Without pollution the air is especially clear and the sun's rays are especially burning. Be prepared with suncream of a suitable strength from the very first day and always have a loose garment on hand to slip on for further protection, especially at the beginning of your holiday. Do not be in a rush, build up your tan slowly; it's better for your skin and it lasts longer.

3. Drink only bottled water and buy the five-litre bottles where possible, it is much cheaper.

4. In order to be able to buy spirits to take home, which are cheaper in shops and supermarkets than at the airport, locate shops which sell them in plastic bottles or take out some rigid plastic bottles. Rigid, leakproof bottles are available from outdoor shops, used by hikers. Plastic bottles can then be packed in the middle of suitcases. Just make sure they are well protected.

5. Whenever you visit a local market, stock up with fresh fruit; it is usually the cheapest place to buy it.

6. Beware of buying branded watches from street sellers, as many are counterfeit.

to support alternative crops. It proved very timely for the demise of the wine industry was on the horizon. Oidium, a fungal disease affecting the vines, arrived on the island in 1853. It originated in North America, and spread to Europe and Spain around 1845 before arriving in the Canaries. The death blow came later, in 1878, with the arrival of another new disease, mildew. Strangely, phylloxera, which devastated Europe's vines in the mid-19th century, never reached the Canaries.

One of the alternative crops introduced in 1825-26 was the prickly pear, *Opuntia ficus indica,* with its attendant parasite *Dactylopius coccus,* more familiarly known as cochineal. Production of the carmine dye from this insect reached a peak about halfway through the 19th century but the introduction of synthetic dyes killed the trade and it was gradually replaced by bananas, tomatoes and potatoes. Bananas were the mainstay of the economy by the end of that century.

The Good Life

Prosperity through wine and from its free trade advantages brought wealthy traders and merchants to settle on Tenerife. They built fine houses and elegant mansions with cool, inner courtyards and some of the island's finest architecture dates from that period. One of the outstanding examples is the House of Balconies (Casa de los Balcones) in La Orotava with its extraordinarily beautiful carved wooden balconies. Tales of the kind climate and the cosmopolitan lifestyle spread to Europe and the 19th century saw a succession of travellers visiting

the island, from artists and scholars to scientists and tourists. Artist Elizabeth Murray painted evocative landscapes which attracted much interest back in England while Alexander von Humboldt, a German scientist and geographer, wrote his account of Tenerife in *From the Orinoco to the Amazon* in 1889. He wrote: 'Anyone who has a feeling for the beauty of nature will find on this delightful island a remedy even more powerful than the climate. No place in the world seems to me more likely than Tenerife and Madeira to banish melancholy and restore peace to a troubled spirit'. Before the end of that century, Tenerife was entertaining something in the region of 500 tourists a year drawn from the wealthy classes of Europe.

Twentieth century

In 1912 the islands were granted self-government and the Cabildos Insulares (Island Councils) were established. Only two years later, with the onset of the First World War, the banana trade was destroyed at a stroke, forcing many Canarians to emigrate to South America, to Venezuela and Cuba in particular. Little was done to ease the economic plight of the Canary Islands, especially since Spain had problems of her own with the uprising of Franco in 1936 and the start of the Civil War. General Francisco Franco was commander of the military region of the Canaries and it was on Tenerife that the military coup was planned.

A new era for Tenerife started in 1959 with the start of charter flights bringing tourists to the island. Los Rodeos in the north was the only airport then

Welcome to Tenerife

and Puerto de la Cruz rapidly developed into an international resort. Even under Franco the Canaries were able to maintain their free trade status and, with more flights to the island, Tenerife was able to establish new markets for their tomatoes, potatoes and cut flowers.

The progress of tourism had a huge setback on 26 March 1977 when Los Rodeos airport was the scene of one of the world's most serious aeroplane crashes in which 577 were killed. Only one year later a new airport, Reina Sofia, opened in the south, offering much higher safety standards.

On 1 January 1986 Spain became a member of the EU, and with it the Canary Islands, but special concessions were permitted for the Canaries regarding their free trade status. Customs regulations allow travellers within the EU to bring in reasonable amounts of wines and spirits which are duty paid. On Tenerife, all wine and spirits purchased in the shops are duty-free, thus the duty-free allowance is restricted.

1. Touring and Exploring

Opposite: Puerto de Santiago

Adeje prom, new section, an extension of Playa da las Américas

Resort Guide

The following gives a thumbnail of the main resorts to help in making the most suitable choice. For more details see the chapter 2 (p33-37) and the Good Beach Guide. Going clockwise from El Médano near the airport:

El Médano

This small resort is developing around an old fishing village close to the airport. Apart from possible aircraft noise, it is quiet with plenty of Spanish character and access to the best natural beach on the island. It has also become a favourite place for windsurfers, suggesting that this could be a rather windy corner.

House, Puerto de la Cruz

Costa del Silencio

Holidays here are centred on the Ten-Bel holiday village, a collection of apartments and bungalows set amongst neat gardens just inland from the coast. There are no beaches immediately to hand but the holiday village provides seawater swimming pools and plenty of facilities for sport and recreation. Here is also the location of San Miguel Marina.

Los Cristianos

Immediately adjacent to Playa de las Américas and connected by a pedestrianised promenade, Los Cristianos has the benefit of starting life as a small fishing port. Development has long since swamped the older section and it is now a large resort, second only to Playa de las Américas. It is quite different in character to the latter, a little quieter and generally appealing to a different clientele. There is life enough near the front which has a wide choice of restaurants and bars while the port is a hive of activity with fishing boats, pleasure craft and ferries coming and going on their daily run to La Gomera. There are beaches along the promenade.

The promenade has long connected with Playa de las Américas and now stretches even further along the coast to La Caleta.

Playa de las Américas

Springing up in the 1960s, this is easily the largest resort on the island and purpose-built for tourism. Bright and lively all summer, it calms down a little in winter when the golden oldies take their holidays. Searching out restaurants, cafés, fast food places, pubs, bars and discos takes no time at all; the place abounds with them. The marina at Puerto Colón forms the heart of the resort while there are a number of beaches spreading either side but there is hardly room to spread a towel at peak times. This is a very international resort but totally lacking in Spanish character and genuine Spanish or Canarian restaurants are very hard to find. Those looking for all the benefits of a large resort but without the full bustle might consider Costa Adeje, on the northern edge of town.

Costa Adeje

The coast between Torviscas/Fañabé and La Caleta is fast developing into a more upmarket resort. A stroll along this stretch of the promenade is a more restful experience, with the occasional café and perhaps lunch in one of the fish restaurants at La Caleta at the end. The really energetic can continue along the coast on a path as far as Playa Paraiso.

Playa Paraiso

A purpose-built developing resort in a surprisingly isolated location on a rocky stretch of coastline with only the tiniest of beaches. Behind the beach, on an inlet, is a man-made pool and sun bathing area. It is a mix of high and low rise buildings but quite self-contained with a good selection of eating places and supporting shops. Be sure that your chosen accommodation has a swimming pool. A bus connects to Playa de las Américas.

Puerto de Santiago

Growing as a large resort around an old village with plenty of character and facilities. It has an extensive beach of the blackest sand imaginable.

Los Gigantes

Built down the hillside and framed by formidable black cliffs, Los Gigantes is very striking. A hilly resort with plenty of shopping facilities. The beach is only small and the surf generally low but the larger beach at Puerto Santiago is within easy reach.

Puerto de la Cruz

Popular long before Playa de las Américas sprang up in the 1960s, Puerto de la Cruz is a resort of great charm. Built down the hillside, it is full of narrow streets and interesting architecture with plenty of tourist attractions around including Loro Parque. There is an extensive beach with the addition of an attractive lido offering a variety of swimming pools. One of the few resorts where the Spanish character has not yielded to international influences.

Good Beach Guide

Much of Tenerife's coastline is rocky but where the cliffs and rocks relent the bays and coves are filled with either jet black or dirty grey-brown sand. Glistening black beaches are uncommon outside volcanic islands and the sight of them often raises a few eyebrows amongst first-time visitors. Imported golden sand has been used to create or improve some beaches and the most

Beach Safety

There is a flag system in operation on most of the major beaches to advise or warn of sea conditions.

Red flag: swimming is highly dangerous and not recommended.

Yellow flag: very strong winds, take extra care.

White/green flag: generally safe for swimming but still exercise care. Swimmers are strongly advised to respect the advice offered.

Since the island is situated in the restless, mobile Atlantic, sea pollution is not generally a problem. A number of beaches have been awarded the EU Blue Flag for sea quality but since this is an annual award, it is important to enquire on the current status.

Jellyfish are not too much of a problem in the seas around Tenerife but it is as well to be aware that they can be encountered. Stings should be treated immediately by cleaning the sting off your skin and applying something cool, ideally an ice pack or perhaps a can of drink direct from the fridge, before using a cream to relieve irritation.

Lido Martianez

spectacular of these is Las Teresitas near Santa Cruz.

Generating new beaches is quite an industry now on the island and there is a high demand for machines to grind down the cinder-type rock into grains of suitable size. It seems certain that new beaches will appear steadily over the next few years. One of the problems with black sand is that it absorbs energy rather too efficiently and it can get very hot in the sun.

On some days the sea rolls in with great breakers and mountains of surf. This is great for the surfers but not so good for less than expert swimmers and certainly dangerous for children. Another problem is the wind. Tenerife lies in the path of the Trade Winds which are normally quite steady and cause no

Teresitas Beach

Playa Jardin, Puerto de la Cruz

discomfort but there are days when the wind is strong enough to blow the sand particles around with some velocity. Many visitors will enjoy a holiday experiencing calm seas and winds but others may not be so lucky. When the seas are running high and the winds are rough, a hotel with a good, sheltered swimming pool and plenty of sunbathing area becomes doubly important.

This is not an exhaustive guide to the beaches on Tenerife, for there are quite a number of tiny bays sheltering a little sand. It is simply a guide to the larger, more popular beaches which may or may not have tourist facilities. Starting from the capital, Santa Cruz, they are presented in a clockwise manner.

Playa de las Teresitas

Located a few miles north of Santa Cruz, this is a superb stretch of fine golden sand, every grain lovingly transported from the Sahara back in the 1970s. Spectacularly located in a

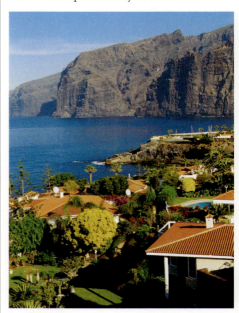
Los Gigantes

sweeping bay backed by green-cloaked hills, it looks so natural that it is hard to appreciate that this is one of the largest man-made beaches in the world. Palm-shaded Teresitas beach is very popular and gets especially crowded in July and August. Parts of the bay here are protected by underwater barriers to prevent the sand being washed away and dispersed but the shallow lagoon created is ideal for children and non-swimmers. Just about every facility is available: plenty of car parking space, a red cross station, toilets and refreshments. Some of the restaurants have a reputation for being excessively over-priced. It has the distinction of being the finest beach on the island.

El Médano

Lying on the southern shore near the airport, this part of the island is windy most of the time and the colourful sails of the windsurfers are a common sight. It is a popular place too for international windsurfing competitions. There are two beaches in town and further beaches just to the west.

Town beach

Yellow-brown sand has been used to make this small beach which provides good bathing when it is not too windy. Sun loungers and parasols are available for hire and there are plenty of refreshment facilities and restaurants immediately behind the beach.

Playa de Médano

The beach lies alongside Hotel Sur Tenerife and slightly east of the town beach. It is joined to the latter by a wooden walkway, with areas for sunbathing. This dark golden brown sandy beach is the larger of the two beaches but less sheltered and not as good for swimming. Expect some noise from the airport.

Playa de la Tejita

Lying to the west of El Médano, this beach is protected by the rocky headland of Montaña Roja. Almost a natural sand colour but darker, this vast expanse of deserted beach has grown in popularity. In spite of the protecting headland, it can still be windy at times. No facilities, except perhaps for a mobile refreshment van at busy times.

Los Cristianos

Los Cristianos has two beaches. The main beach is an extensive sweep of brownish yellow sand which lies to the east of the harbour. It is interrupted by rocks in parts but it is well maintained, kept fairly clean and is good for children. To the rear of the beach lies the pedestrianised walkway which has all the facilities needed in terms of snacks, drinks or ice creams.

The second beach, Playa de las Vistas, lies just to the west of the harbour. It offers a fine expanse of clean sand with an inviting-looking sea.

Vistasur shopping centre marks the end of Los Cristianos and the start of Playa de las Américas. The walkway continues and leads to yet more beaches.

Wheelchair access is very good in Los Cristianos, better than Playa de las Américas.

Playa de las Américas

There is a selection of beaches in Playa de las Américas. The first, after leaving Los Cristianos, is a delightful and popular horseshoe-shaped beach of fine golden sand decked with thatched sun-shades. Directly behind is a two-level walkway with grassy areas for those who prefer to sunbathe on grass. An attractive beach, good for children, with facilities on hand.

Playa Torviscas beach follows Puerto Colon, then the 1.5km/1 mile stretch of Playa de Fañabé. Just beyond, round the headland, the waves at Playa del Duque are an attraction.

Puerto Santiago

Playa de la Arena: one of the island's natural beaches of glistening black sand. Although located in a small cove, the Atlantic rollers here can have a dangerous undertow which makes it unsafe for children and non-swimmers. Otherwise it is an attractive and well-kept beach backed by colourful gardens. Sun loungers and parasols are available and facilities for drinks, snacks or meals are close at hand.

San Marcos

Located just east of Garachico, San Marcos is another beach of black sand which is the holder of a blue flag. This is another beach where it pays to be wary of the sea and its dangerous undercurrents. Plenty of facilities nearby in the form of bars and restaurants.

Los Realejos

Playa de Socorro: yet more black sand and white surf.

This is a very natural beach with virtually no facilities and yet it gets very crowded in July and August. It is a paradise for surfers and occasionally the venue for international competitions.

Puerto de la Cruz

Playa Jardin comprises three adjoining black sand beaches stretching from the fort out as far as Loro Parque. It is man-made but looks entirely natural. Sun loungers and parasols are available and there is a good range of facilities within easy distance. Surfing takes place at the Loro Parque end.

2. Days Out

Opposite: Cailla San Telmo, Puerto de la Cruz
Below: Lemur in the Monkey Park zoo

There is a good selection of theme parks and places of entertainment around Playa de las Américas and Los Cristianos. Some provide free buses but the others are easily reached by a short taxi ride.

A Day Out in La Gomera

Just 32km (20 miles) away from Tenerife and easily visible from the west coast, **La Gomera** remains relatively unspoilt. It is the second smallest island in the group with a population of around 20,000. Distances might seem small, as it is just 23km (14 miles) deep and 25km (15.5 miles) wide, but travelling on the island is hindered by a terrain punctuated by mountains and deep gorges. Roads follow winding routes making the island seem much larger and allowing only slow progress.

While it is simple enough to catch the ferry or hydrofoil from Los Cristianos across to **San Sebastián** on La Gomera, it is not so easy to get around the island without transport. If you already have a hire car you may wish to take it across on the ferry (check with hire company first). Local buses do meet arriving ferries and return again for the evening ferry so it may be possible to visit one of the other major towns on the island, either Valle Gran Rei, Vallehermosa or Playa de Santiago, and see something of the island on the way.

While the ferry takes about an hour and a half, the hydrofoil cuts a dash and reaches the small port and chief town of San Sebastián in around 35 minutes. On arrival, ignore the narrow streets and little white houses climbing the hillside if catching the local bus or a taxi is important and head straight for the laurel shaded main square, Plaza Calvo Sotelo. If there is time to spare, head for the **Church of the Assumption** where Christopher Columbus is supposed to have attended mass in 1492 before setting off into the unknown and discovering Cuba. Casa Colombina is

39

Family Entertainment in the South

Parque Ecologico las Aguilas del Teide

Open 9am–6pm: Free buses are well advertised.

Exotic birds, hippopotamus, crocodiles, kangaroos; there is plenty to keep the family amused. Special shows with the animals are laid on throughout the day but the one not to miss is a demonstration of raptors. Free-flying eagles are exciting enough but the sight of a South American Condor flying in the arena is something again. There are snack bars around and picnic areas for those taking their own food. A challenging jungle assault course provides fun for all ages.

Siam Park

This unique, new and exciting water theme park, part of the Loro Park Group, covers a massive area in Costa Adeje. Enjoy the many different attractions, including sea lions an aquarium and much more. The ultimate attraction must be the Wave Pool, which has a sandy beach and different sized waves, some of which reach a height of 3m/9ft 8ins for surfers. Covering a huge area to the north of the motorway behind the bus station and the Magma Art & Congress Centre.

Aquapark

Open 10am–6pm. This is located to the rear of Playa de las Américas, on the inland side of the motorway in San Eugenio Alto. Free buses from Playa de las Américas and Los Cristianos.

The entry cost covers all the activities although there is an extra charge inside for sunbeds and for use of the dry play area for children. Entry prices are slightly lower after 3pm. There is plenty of watery fun for the family with water chutes and all sorts of slides and rides in addition to the pool.

Exotic Park

Open 10am–6pm. This is located close to the motorway, just north of the exit for Las Galletas. Free buses operate collecting customers from Playa de las Américas and Los Cristianos.

The cactus garden is the main draw here but there are a few animals etc.

Monkey Park (next door to Exotic Park)

A large selection of different species of monkeys is on view here as it is an international breeding centre for endangered species of primates. These are also iguanas, toucans and lemurs, etc. all of which make a visit worthwhile.

Camel Park

Open 10am–5pm. Located off the Arona road just beyond Chayofa. Free buses from Playa de las Américas and Los Cristianos. Book yourself a safari with lunch and sample local wine and produce.

also thought to have some connection with Columbus and the 15th century tower, Torre del Conde. Built in 1447 as part of the town's defences, it was strengthened in the following century to serve as safe storage for booty brought back from America by the Conquistadors.

Like Tenerife it shares the same north-south divide with the south of the island dry and arid with a lower rainfall than both the north and the centre of the island. Again it shows up in the vegetation with the north and the interior lush and green. Less evident are the volcanic forms seen on Tenerife yet it shares the same origins but perhaps from an earlier date. Visions of La Gomera as nothing more than a mound of rock are quickly dispelled when travelling there. Deeply cut by great gorges opening to wide valleys, the mountainous interior is covered by dense forests, pine in the upper regions and laurel at lower levels. It is easy to appreciate how the whistling language (*siblo*) developed here in this difficult terrain. *El siblo*, which is still practised on this island, is used to send messages over long distances across the valleys, even across the length of the island when a chain of people is involved.

With only slow progress possible, the best advice to day trippers is not to plan too adventurous an itinerary and concentrate on fairly simple objectives. One of the more spectacular trips includes Parque Nacional da Garajonay and the viewpoint at La Laguna Grande for breathtaking views of the central mountains. The island is very popular with walkers and *Landscapes of Southern Tenerife and La Gomera* (Noel Rochford, Sunflower Books, London) describes a good selection of walks.

A Day Out at Loro Parque

Situated on the outskirts of Puerto de la Cruz, the award-winning **Loro Parque** is one of the island's top attractions, providing fun for the whole family. It has grown steadily since it first opened to the public in 1972 and now covers 12.5 hectares (31 acres), housing some 300 species and subspecies of parrots in a tropical garden paradise along with countless animals.

It opens at 8.30am and closes at 5pm which is probably just enough time to see everything there is to see as well as taking in the shows. There is a free train departing from Martiánez Beach in the centre of Puerto de la Cruz every 20 minutes. Should the queue for the train be too long, it is only a short taxi ride and it may be even quicker to walk than wait 20 minutes for the next train. For visitors arriving by car, there is plenty of parking space.

Entry leads straight into the Thai Village which was crafted in Thailand and constructed on site. Inspired by a Thai temple, the main pavilion houses a large conference room but there is a souvenir shop and other services. Outside, the smaller Thai building contains a museum of porcelain devoted to parrots and the adjoining lake contains a shoal of Japanese koi carp. From here the day needs careful planning for there is so much to see and do. The first thing is to check the times of the shows, all of which are worth seeing. These include the very popular dolphin show in which six dolphins demonstrate their

Tenerife

Loro Parque sea lions

Days Out

Loro Parque dolphins

skills and abilities with seeming enjoyment, the parrot show with free-flying macaws, the Loro show with cockatoos and macaws showing off on scooters and the sea lion show for another aquatic display of awesome swimming and diving power.

Orcas whales are the latest attraction and it's amazing to see these huge mammals happily play to the crowd. Beware though, if you're sitting in the front few rows, as you may be in for an unexpected watery surprise.

The shows are repeated several times each day but they are held in different places and it does take time to move around the site since idling visitors enjoying the exhibits hinder progress. In between these shows, there are plenty of other distractions like the gorilla jungle, the bat cave, tiger island, an underwater tunnel through the heart of the shark pool and an arctic penguin house. Add the parrots, other exotic birds like the flamingoes, aquariums, an orchidarium displaying 1,000 flowers, endless borders of exotic flowers, 2,000 palm trees and it is enough to absorb as much time as can be allowed.

Picnic areas are provided for those taking their own food and there are plenty of snack bars around serving both food and drink. An adventure

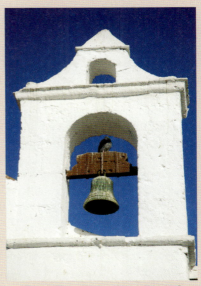

Cailla San Telmo, Puerto de la Cruz

playground gives the children the opportunity to work off some steam when tired of spectating and there is a grill restaurant for serious eaters.

Loro Parque has a scientific side too. It has been heavily involved in the care and conservation of parrots since it first opened and has developed the finest breeding centre in the world. A fully equipped clinic staffed by veterinarians takes care of every aspect of the health of the birds and biologists help with dietary aspects. In 1992 the Loro Parque Foundation was created for the purpose of preserving psittacines (parrots) in danger of extinction. It is a non-profit-making organisation and the funds raised are used for field studies and conservation projects, research and educational campaigns. The Foundation now has an Eco-Shop selling videos, T-shirts and souvenirs

Bananera El Guanche

In their natural state, bananas are a jungle weed of great diversity most prolific in the Burma–New Guinea region but a small species of banana, *Musa cavendishii*, from Indochina showed that it could flourish in the wetter parts of the island. By 1890 it was well established and rapidly filling a void in the economy. Although small it is very tasty but its qualities were not good enough for it to withstand competition from the larger bananas of Central and South America. The Spanish government guaranteed the market for the Canarian banana and took virtually the whole crop while excluding bananas from other countries. However, this protection disappeared with Spain's entry into the EU and, after a period of transition, regulations were changed to allow a free market. Tenerife is back in crisis over its banana trade.

Like Bananera Atlantic Gardens near Los Cristianos, Bananera El Guanche at Puerto de la Cruz takes the trouble to illustrate the cultural requirements and the life cycle of this plant. It dismisses a common fallacy that, despite its size, the banana is not a tree but a plant. It does not have a true trunk and is no more than a powerfully growing shoot which dies back once it has borne fruit. Fortunately, it sends out several suckers from beneath the ground and the strongest is selected and allowed to mature to produce the next crop. In the kind climate on Tenerife, bananas grow all year round, producing a crop every seven months. The plant produces a flowering spike from the centre which has female flowers clustering the base with male flowers grouped around the end. As the flowers open, the stigma (pistil) is removed from the female flower from which the banana develops and the pod of male flowers at the end is cut off. Within 4 to 7 months the stem of bananas, which may weigh 15 to 18kg (33–40lbs), is ready to harvest and is usually cut while the fruit is still green, just before it is ready to eat.

Apart from wandering around the banana plantation at Bananera El Guanche, which includes a free banana and a sample of banana liqueur, there is also a garden of tropical trees and plants and a cactus garden with over 400 specimens.

Days Out

and anyone interested in joining the Foundation can apply at the shop.

A Day Out in Puerto de la Cruz

As one of the older and more fashionable towns on the island, Puerto de la Cruz oozes character. It existed long before tourism, attracting its share of rich and wealthy settlers largely on account of its proximity to the fertile Orotava Valley. It was founded early in the 17th century as a fishing village and a small port exporting sugar grown around La Orotava and was known originally as Puerto de la Orotava. It developed significantly after the earthquake of 1706 which destroyed Garachico, the main port for the wine trade at that time, and Puerto de la Cruz took over much of this trade. By the end of the 19th century, wealthy Britons and Europeans were discovering its charms and mild winter climate and creating a demand for hotels and guest houses. The real boom in tourism happened in the mid-20th century when Puerto de la Cruz developed into the island's most important international resort before being eclipsed by Playa de las Américas and Los Cristianos for the top spot, but it still hosts many thousands of visitors each year and remains a premier resort. Down on the seafront is a magnificent lido so be sure to pack a swimming costume and shoppers beware, Puerto de la Cruz could cause serious damage to your holiday funds, as it offers the best shopping on the island next to Santa Cruz.

Three roads lead into town from the autopista and, if arriving by car, the simplest entry point is the most northerly of these, signposted 'Jardin Botánico'. Very shortly, on the left, is a banana plantation, **Bananera El Guanche**, which is open to the public (from 9am–6pm, see p44) and has parking space outside. A free bus service brings visitors up from the promenade so this could be left until later, if preferred.

Immediately beyond Bananera El Guanche fork off right following signs to the **Botanical Garden** (small entry fee) located on the right soon after the junction. Founded by King Charles III of Spain in the 18th century, the idea was to introduce and establish tropical plants to the more temperate climate of Tenerife as a first step prior to their introduction to mainland Spain. While the garden flourished on Tenerife, the transfer of acclimatised plants to Spain was much less successful. The garden is not exceptionally large, covering an area of only 2.4 hectares (6 acres), but contains more than 200 specimens of trees, shrubs and plants from all over the world. Within the space of half an hour oceans can be crossed and new continents visited in the form of coffee plants, breadfruit trees, tulip trees, mangoes and exotic orchids in the hothouse.

Shopping precincts beyond the garden mark the build-up of **Puerto de la Cruz**. Much of the town occupies the lower and flatter part of the hillside by the coast.

Park at the top of Calle de Aguilar y Quesada – go left as the dual carrageway ends into a multi-storey car park.

Puerto de la Cruz is an absorbing maze of pedestrianised walkways, palm trees, wooden Canarian balconies, old houses of character and pavement cafés. Perhaps the best place to start a

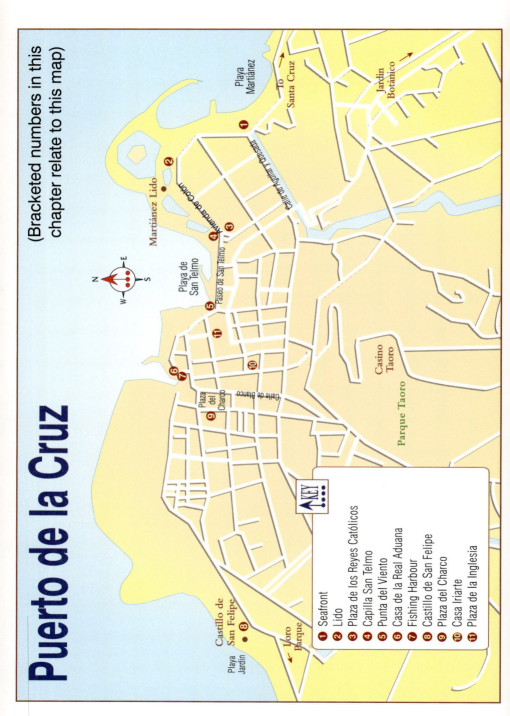

Family Entertainment in the North

Loro Parque

Puerto de la Cruz (open 8.30am–5pm). A free train collects visitors from the centre of Puerto de la Cruz. Fully described on p41, this parrot park and zoo set in tropical surroundings is the island's top attraction which tour operators offer as an organised day out.

Parrots at Loro Parque

Lido Martiánez

Puerto de la Cruz (open all day, every day). A man-made outdoor complex of eight swimming pools set amongst exotic plants and flowers. Loads of space for sunbathing and relaxing with plenty of facilities on hand.

Oasis del Valle

El Ramal, by junction 33, La Orotava (open 10am–5pm). Free buses leave Café Columbus, Puerto de la Cruz every 20 minutes. Zoo animals set in exotic gardens, camel rides, café bar and excellent restaurants serving typical Canarian food. Slowly changing from a small zoo into a Canarian wildlife park but an excellent lunch stop regardless.

Camello

El Tanque, near Icod de los Vinos (open 10am–6pm). Dress as an Arab and enjoy a camel safari, departing every 15 minutes, and finish with Arabian tea.

Casa del Vino la Baranda

An attraction for families with older children. Once part of a 17th century estate, now the Tenerife Vine and Wine Museum. Taste wine and visit the museums of wine and honey. Lunch in the restaurant or sample local specialities sitting in the sun on the terrace or in the bar. Exit the motorway Junction 25 at El Sauzal and follow signs to Cas del Vino; only a few hundred yards. Open Tue–Sun. Closed Mon. Summer Tue 11.30–19.30 (10.30–18.30 winter); Wed–Sat 10.00–21.30; Sun 11.00–18.00.

Camel trek, Camello

walkabout is at the **seafront** (1) where traffic heads inland into Calle de Aguillar y Quesada. Stroll along Avenida de Colon, where sketch artists, painters and souvenir sellers add to the colour, passing the **Martiánez Lido (2).**

Designed by César Manrique and finished in 1977, the lido is a beautifully arranged complex of eight blue swimming pools and lakes set on different levels with islands and bridges. Palm trees, artificial white beaches and brightly coloured flowers lend a touch of the exotic but, on the practical side, sunbathing areas are generous and well sheltered, there is good swimming for all ages and abilities and refreshments are never too far away. There is even a subterranean nightclub, the Andromeda, with a restaurant and nightly floorshows.

Views inland from the front sometimes open up to show the dominant building of Casino Taoro perched on a hilltop in **Parque Taoro**. It is around this park area where the British expatriates chose to settle and where many still live.

The small square you can now reach is the **Plaza de los Reyes Católicos** (3) which is named after the Catholic Monarch Ferdinand of Aragon (1479–1516) who married the Catholic Isabel of Castile in 1469. It was during their reign that Tenerife was conquered by Spain.

On the right at the start of Paseo de San Telmo is the small white chapel, **Capilla San Telmo** (4), which was built by fishermen in 1626 and dedicated to their patron saint San Telmo (St Elmo). It has been through fire (1778) and tempest (1826) and suffered numer-

ous restorations, the latest in 1968. The original statute of San Pedro González Telmo was lost in the fire and its replacement was made in 1783.

A small square at the end of Paseode San Telmo, known as **Punta del Viento** (5), has a terrace offering fine coastal views accompanied by the roar of the sea crashing against the rocks below.

Stay along the coastline now to the old fishing harbour (7). The large yellow stone house here is **Casa de la Real Aduana** (6), now the Tourist Information Centre. It is the oldest surviving building in Puerto, which served as the customs house from 1706 to 1833.

A ten minute diversion from the fishing harbour (7) along the front to the west leads to the town's early fortifications, **Castillo de San Felipe** (8), built early in the 17th century on the orders of King Felipe IV. It was he who instigated the foundation of La Orotava and its port, Puerto de la Orotava (now Puerto de la Cruz). Beyond here are the glistening black beaches of Playa Jardin which were made by crushing rock to a fine particle size to resemble sand. Loro Parque lies at the far end.

Head inland a short distance now to the heart of the town and the lively **Plaza del Charco** (9), full of locals and visitors enjoying a drink or animated conversation beneath the shade of Indian laurels. This is a meeting point, the social heart of the town during the day and early evening. Calle Puerto Viejo, leading off to the west from the inland corner, is where the locals head to find a fish restaurant.

Wander inland from the Plaza, on the left-hand side, along Calle de Blanco and turn left into Calle Iriarte, as the pedestrianised section ends. Traditional wooden balconies can be seen along many of the streets in the old part of town and many newer properties still follow this tradition but there are some attractive balconies along this street typified by **Casa Iriarte** (10) located on the junction with Calle San Juan. It is an 18th century mansion now used as a souvenir shop but there is a naval museum on the top floor with a few model ships and naval bits for the enthusiasts. Rather more fascinating is the inner courtyard. Stepped streets overhung with balconies and shaded by cool green palms are where locals and visitors alike are happy to rest awhile and let the world go by.

Turn left, seawards, opposite Casa Iriarte into Calle San Juan. On reaching Calle de Quintana turn right uphill. A left here leads back into Plaza del Charco.

Reach the large **Plaza de la Inglesia** (11) shaded by palms and brightened by flower beds. Dominating the square is the church of **Nuestra Señora de la Peña de Francia**, the town's most important church which was built in the early 17th century and features a fine baroque retable by Luis de la Cruz and an organ brought from London in 1814 by Bernardo de Cologán, a Canary Islander of Irish descent.

Stay along Calle de Quintana back to the coast at Punta del Viento where a right leads downhill, between the shops and the sea, along Paseo de San Telmo and back to the start of the walk.

A Day Out in Santa Cruz

Santa Cruz, or more correctly Santa Cruz de Tenerife, lies in a sheltered bay at the foot of the Anaga mountains and is the capital of the island. It is a major port, one of Spain's largest, thanks to its position on important Atlantic sea routes. Although the town does attract visitors, it has significant industrial sections which include an oil refinery, chemical plant and other factories. About one third of the island's population lives here.

In spite of all its commercial and industrial aspects, the town does have some charm, albeit a little faded, and the best shopping on the island. Parking is a major problem which eases by mid-afternoon when offices close. There is parking right on the front near the centre but it fills very early. Sightseers can take their time but shoppers should make an early start since the market and many of the shops close at 1pm for the afternoon, although major stores like Maya in the centre and El Corte Inglés near the bus station stay open all day. If there is time left at the end of the day there are two options for a swim, either the spectacular beach of Playa de las Teresitas or the Parque Maritimo Lido with its seawater swimming pools near the bus station.

Santa Cruz was nothing more than an uninhabited bay back in 1492 but it was the place that Fernández de Lugo chose to land when he led his troops in the conquest of the island for Spain. The town was founded by him in 1492 but it was not, at that stage, the capital nor did it develop significantly as a port until after the volcanic eruption in 1706 which destroyed the port of Garachico. It became the capital of the island and the administrative centre for the whole of the Canary Islands in

Carnival

Carnival (*Carnaval*) on Tenerife is an event not to be missed. It is huge, colourful, noisy, imaginative, good-natured, second only to Mardi Gras in Rio de Janeiro and ranking alongside the carnivals in New Orleans or Notting Hill. It is the main event of the year starting first in Santa Cruz sometime in February before moving around the island, first to Puerto de la Cruz then on to Los Cristianos about the middle of March. The date varies according to the start of Lent; in fact the word carnival is said to derive from the Italian word *carnivale* meaning the removing of meat.

Each year Carnival follows a different theme; Ancient Egypt, Disneyland and Mexico have been used in recent years. As soon as the theme for the next carnival is known, groups spend months designing their costumes and choreographing their dance routines. Miles of material are consumed and millions of sequins sewn into place before the big day arrives. While the Grand Procession is clearly the highlight, there are many events in the week before, including choosing the Carnival Queen and, of course, the Carnival Ball. The ritual end to the carnival, usually the day after the main parade, is the Burial of the Sardine where 'widows' mourn the death of a giant sardine.

This good-natured, lively event has in fact become a huge draw attracting as many as 200,000 visitors so it can be difficult to book a holiday or find accommodation on the island for that period. Vendors are out in force selling drinks, sweets, doughnuts (*churros*), kebabs (*pinchitos*), flags, streamers, hats and just about everything else. Street entertainers perform for the waiting crowds before the Latin American rhythms strike up and the flamboyant dancers and musicians rumba their way along the route starting a procession of floats, dancers, bands of riotous colour, noise and movement which may take a couple of hours to pass.

Days Out

New auditorium in Santa Cruz

1726. Since 1927, when the Canaries were divided into two provinces, Santa Cruz administers only La Gomera, El Hierro and La Palma.

Its existence has not been entirely peaceful. Admiral Blake tried to take the

Balconies in Puerto de la Cruz

town in 1657 but failed, as did Admiral Jennings in the War of the Spanish Succession in 1706. Perhaps the most famous failed attack was that of Nelson himself in 1797 who lost his right arm in the attempt.

In spite of the island's huge success in attracting tourism, Santa Cruz is not really part of this scene but there is one occasion in the year when its hotels are bursting at the seams: Carnival (see p50). This is when the town really lets its hair down and parties in style.

The natural place to start a tour is in Plaza España, right in the centre of town on the seafront which is recognised by the huge circular **Monumento de los Caidos** commemorating the dead of the Spanish Civil War. It is in fact a memorial chapel and a lift ascends the towering cross but it is only used on special occasions. The views from the top must be spectacular with the Anaga mountains so close. The tourist office is located in the Palacio Insular, the large building to the south, and picking up a town plan here may be the best way to start.

Since the market, **Mercado de Nuestra Señora de Africa**, closes at 1pm, it perhaps should be the first port of call. It is a ten-minute walk away, reached by heading southwards along Avenida de Bravo Murillo, then cutting inland along Calle de San Sebastián. Take a moment along the way to enjoy traditional coloured house façades in the side streets off to the right. Stalls outside sell all sorts of goods from clothing to souvenirs but the main market is entered through the huge arch. Quality and prices here are the best on the island.

Head back now to Plaza Español to continue on this tour before the shops close. If the tourist train is waiting, it is tempting to join it for a brief sightseeing trip. Leading inland directly from the Plaza Español is the pedestrianised Plaza de la Candelaria. Banks and commercial buildings surround this elongated square but it does house shaded café tables and a few shops. Dominant in the centre is the statue representing the **Triumph of the Virgin of Candelaria** (El Triunfo de la Candelaria) which was sculpted by the renowned Italian sculptor Antonio Canova (1757–1822) and erected in 1778. The Virgin of Candelaria is the patron saint of the whole Canary Islands (see p68). Here she is seen perched on top of a needle, child in one arm and a candle in the other hand, while four Guanche kings pay homage below.

Serious shopping starts on entering the pedestrianised Calle de Castillo, the town's main shopping street. Gypsies selling embroidered tablecloths are very much part of the street life. Not all the cloths on offer are Canarian; many are cheap imports. One shop where genuine embroidered linen can be found is **La Casa de los Balcones**, an outlet from the embroidery school of La Orotava, where women can be seen busily embroidering.

Art lovers may be interested in visiting the **Museo Municipal de Bellas Artes** (open 10am–7.30pm), at Calle José Murphy 4, just off to the right. It holds a collection of paintings and sculptures both local and international and is housed in a former Franciscan friary.

Santa Cruz's important monuments and places of interest are mostly churches and museums. The archaeological museum lies close to the town's most important church, **Nuestra Señora de la Concepción**.

To find them both, head off from Plaza España along Avenida de Bravo Murillo, just inland from the coast road. First encountered is the church of Nuestra Señora de la Concepción in Plaza de la Iglesia, easily recognised by its tiered bell tower which is quite a landmark. Built in 1502, it is one of the two oldest churches on the island and the most important. It was extensively restored during the 17th and 18th centuries. Just beyond the church, also on the right, is the museum (open 10am–8pm, Sunday (free entry) 10am–2pm, closed Monday). It houses a comprehensive exhibition including archaeology, Guanche history, natural science, marine history, anthropology and culture.

To finish off the day, visitors now

Days Out

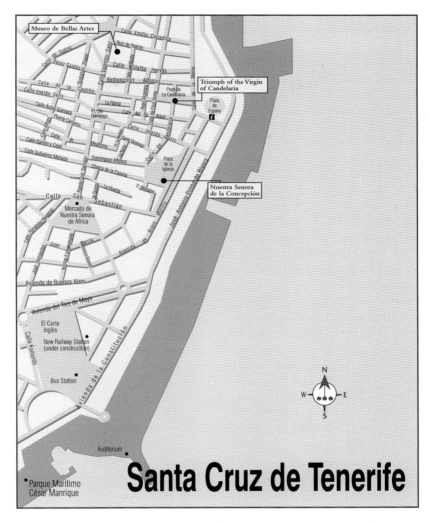

Santa Cruz de Tenerife

have a choice. A ten-minute walk south from Plaza España leads to the **Parque Marítimo Lido** designed by César Manrique whose work has been much admired. He was the architect behind the highly successful Martiánez Lido at Puerto de la Cruz but, sadly, he died in a car accident in 1992. Present facilities include large seawater pools, a beach reclaimed from the sea, snack bars, changing rooms and shops. It is located just beyond the white auditorium reminiscent of the opera house at Sydney.

The alternative is to catch a bus (no. 910 to S. Andrés) for the short ride out to the spectacular **Playa de las Teresitas** beach framed by the Anaga mountains. It is the perfect complement to the bustle of city life and a delightful way to spend the rest of the day.

53

3. Car Tours

Opposite: Masca

All the car tours are designed with Playa de las Américas and Los Cristianos in mind as the starting point, mainly because this area hosts the vast majority of the island's visitors. It should not be too difficult for tourists staying in other resorts to plan their own entry point into the tour in most cases.

The Silent South

For years nothing happened on the southern tip of the island and it earned itself the name of Costa del Silencio. Dry and arid, it was too much of a challenge for the farmers, especially when the north offered much more favourable conditions. This mattered little to the fishermen so small traditional villages developed around the coast, happily living in isolation while pursuing a timeless lifestyle. Change started with the building of the international airport, which brought noise if nothing else, and with the development of Playa de las Américas and Los Cristianos. Suddenly, these villages have been noticed and are attracting holidaymakers and developers.

This tour explores the Costa del Silencio and visits villages such as Las Galletas, Los Abrigos and El Médano but there are some good beaches encountered along the way. Most of the eating places in the villages are typical Canarian restaurants, mainly serving fish, so there will be no problem over lunch. Very little driving is involved for those staying in Playa de las Américas or Los Cristianos.

Starting out from Playa de las Américas or Los Cristianos, take the motorway heading for Santa Cruz and leave at the first junction past Los Cristianos, junction 26, signposted San Lourenzo and Guaza and head seawards. Guaza, the first village, is a hotchpotch of industrial buildings interspersed with tapas bars and restaurants straggling along the road. Beyond here golf courses associated with timeshare complexes are rapidly filling the landscape. Keep following signs for **Las Galletas**, which is soon reached. An old fishing village character still dominates and the harbour here is full of fishing boats but the sight of a modern yacht is no longer remarkable. Fishermen sorting out their nets or just engaged in deep conversation while puffing away on cigarettes is about as much activity as can be expected around the port but there is always a chance that a boat may arrive or depart. Beyond the harbour is a short promenade overlooking a sand and shingle beach where most of the fish restaurants are to be found. Old fishermen's houses are tucked away and masked by modern apartment blocks but it is still possible to find a small café close to the sea edge to enjoy a quiet drink.

To make onward progress from here, head inland towards the motorway but do not join it; turn south following signs to Los Abrigos. **Los Abrigos** has built up something of a reputation for its fish restaurants which cluster around the port. There are plenty, and some in enviable positions, but this is not the cheapest place to eat fish.

Once beyond Los Abrigos, the road leads towards El Médano. There are a number of tracks leading off the road heading seaward along here, some of them ideal for finding a quiet picnic spot. Encountered first before entering El Médano is the large beach of **Playa de la Tejita**, one of the best natural beaches on the island, guarded by the imposing headland of Montaña Roja. In its more deserted days, this beach was favoured for nude bathing. Although a windy corner of the island, it has its good days and the beach is popular even though there is nothing in the way of facilities. El Médano, reached very shortly, is developing into a large holiday resort, despite its close proximity to the airport. First encountered is an area of sand dunes from where **El Médano**, meaning sand dunes or sandbank, takes its name. It catches the wind, much to the delight of the windsurfers, and is often used for competitions. Here too is Hotel Playa Sur Tenerife and there is a boardwalk from the hotel to the main town beach which is attractively enclosed and backed by a pedestrianised promenade littered by pavement cafés. Although there is no great depth of sand, the beach is more sheltered and popular with families.

Steps from the beach lead into the main square but the village is only small so there is not too much to see.

From El Médano the road leads inland back to the motorway and to Los Cristianos and Playa de las Américas.

Teide National Park

This is the classic tour on Tenerife which nobody wishes to miss. The park itself includes the very peak of the mountain, Pico de Teide, and the surrounding area known as Caldeira del Cañadas which together form the central region of the island. Often the summit is not visible from the starting point and it is not always possible to assess the weather conditions at the top. To make sure the Teleférico (cable car) is operating, check by telephone on ☎ 922 010 440. It operates from 9am to 4pm. Anyone wishing to walk the final 170m (550ft) to the top will require a permit; enquire at the Park Office, 5 Calle Calzadilla, Santa Cruz.

Las Cañadas del Teide is a giant volcanic crater lying below and close to the mountain peak itself. Huge in size with a diameter of some 16km (10 miles), it is surrounded by high rock walls and the whole was once part of a higher peak before the crater collapsed. Within the crater are great masses of solidified lava and weird rock formations in a wide range of colours. Largely free of soil and vegetative cover, it really is a spectacular lunar landscape.

This particular tour uses the route from Playa de las Américas, explores las Cañadas and returns via Los Gigantes, exploring some coastal resorts

Walking Hell's Valley
(Barranco del Infierno)

Barranco del Infierno is one of the most popular walks on the island. There is an entry charge and the number of walkers is limited to 200 per day. Reservations ☎ 922 782 885. It starts from the village of Adeje in the south of the island, about 8km (5 miles) from Playa de las Américas from which there is a regular bus service (nos 416, 417 and 473). The village itself is small but interesting with plenty of snack bars and restaurants so the best plan is to start out as early as possible to avoid the heat and get back in time for lunch. Although the walk starts on a good path, it gets rocky further up the valley and sensible walking shoes are essential. Care and at least normal agility is needed in the final section where the valley narrows and the small river has to be crossed several times. In length the walk is around 8km (5 miles) but the going is slow in parts so allow about 4 hours although regular walkers might well take less time. It is important to carry some drinking water.

If arriving by car, drive to the top of the village and turn up the road signposted 'Barranco' which may be recognised by the cannon on the junction. The path starts at the top by a restaurant bar. Walkers arriving by bus will have to walk up through the village to find the start, which may take 20–30 minutes.

Follow the path signposted by the restaurant which very quickly gives a view into the ravine. Typical vegetation of dry slopes, the prickly pear cactus, *Opuntia ficus indica*, and *Euphorbia* species are common here but these slowly give way to species which enjoy a little shade and damp as the walk progresses. One speciality of the island's flora to look out for on this walk is the Canarian bellflower, *Canarina canariensis*, which scrambles over other bushes.

Route finding is no problem; all that is necessary is to follow the path as it penetrates the gorge. Eventually, the path zigzags down to the river bed which is crossed. For much of the season this river carries little water but that changes in winter after rains when the walk becomes a little more challenging since the path crosses and recrosses the river several times before the waterfall at the end is reached. Here the water tumbles some 80m (260ft) into a small pool although it can hardly be called spectacular, but the main satisfaction is that it represents the end of the walk. The return is by the outward route.

on the return. There is a total ascent of some 2,300m (7,550ft) by road but there are no especially steep gradients, nor sections close to steep drops. The road does twist and turn so be prepared for a slow and steady drive. The tour which follows (p62) uses the same upward route but returns by the Orotava Valley.

Leave Playa de las Américas on the road signposted San Lorenzo and Arona and, once through Chayofa, turn left towards Arona. The road continues to climb steadily through the hillsides painted white with chrysanthemums in spring and skirts around **Arona**. It is possible to drive through the town and pick the road up again but be warned, the streets are narrow with limited opportunities for parking. The parish church stands in a square in the centre of town and is surrounded by houses with traditional wooden balconies.

As the road continues on its upward zigzag, there are good views briefly down on Los Cristianos and shortly a camera sign indicates a stopping place with views down over Playa de las Américas and Los Cristianos. The tree line is reached somewhere around here

Calderia del Cañadas

Mount Teide

58

Car Tours

where conditions are no longer too dry and the pine trees can survive.

On the approach to **Vilaflor**, be sure to take the road off left to Teide unless the village itself is to be visited. It has the distinction of being the highest village on the island, perhaps in the Canaries, situated at a height of 1,161m (3,809ft) and perhaps most famous for its spring water, bottled and sold around the island, and for its lace-work. Although an agricultural centre, Vilaflor is a pretty village full of little white houses but, ambience apart, there is little of interest except perhaps for the church of San Pedro in the upper village square and the ruins of an old monastery. There is a tourist market held every Sunday between 9am and 4pm, except in bad weather.

A mirador just above Vilaflor, famous for its huge pine tree, Pino Gordo, has

Teide National Park

59

been extended to incorporate picnic facilities. It is an excellent viewpoint with especially good views down over Vilaflor. From hereon the road continues in an almost gentle ascent, twisting and turning through superb scenery. The ease of reaching the seemingly level ground of las Cañadas comes almost as a surprise.

Stay straight ahead on reaching the Boca de Tauce road junction but note that the road left to Los Gigantes here is eventually the onward route. The intention now is to drive over las Cañadas to experience its unrivalled landscape dominated by the towering peak of Mount Teide as far as the information centre and then return to this point to continue. Visitors intending to ride up to the summit are unlikely to have enough time to complete the full tour.

Take heart, the last volcanic eruption in this area occurred in 1798 and Teide is now regarded as quiescent with just the possibility of an eruption of sulphurous gasses or hot mud. Some of the areas and rock formations here have their own names and the first of these is the flat area on the left known as the Llano (plain) de Ucana which sometimes transforms into a small lake with the snowmelt at the end of winter. Just a little further along the road is an area of blue-green rocks known as Los Azulejos and beyond, forming a boundary to the lake area is a spiny backbone of volcanic rocks known as **Los Roques de García**, one of the park's most spectacular sights. Lying close to the road, it is a great stopping place for cars and coaches so Los Roques is often covered with great swarms of tourists climbing up to a high viewpoint. Across the road from Los Roques is the Parador de Cañadas del Teide.

Footpaths exist to lead hardy walkers to the summit of Teide but most people will be content to use the cable car (El Teleférico) reached shortly. At the top of the cable car is a refuge with a bar and from there a footpath leads up to the summit in around 30–40 minutes. Walking can be difficult even for the fit because of the lack of oxygen at this altitude and some may feel light-headed or dizzy. If this is accompanied by sickness, the best plan is to go back down when the symptoms should disappear. People with heart conditions are not advised to climb to the top.

Every corner now reveals new and unexpected vistas unique to this rare and beautiful volcanic landscape. Much further on, at the eastern entrance to the park, is the **El Portillo** information and visitor centre which has a small exhibition about the National Park and an information area.

Take the road back across las Cañadas, enjoying the landscape again from a different perspective. Turn right for Los Gigantes on reaching the road junction. It is like driving through the spent cinders from a giant boiler for a short while. Although the road does wind and twist at times, it is not as challenging to the driver as the upward route and leads down very quickly. Take care on reaching the village at Chio to find the Tamaimo road, especially since the road through Arguayo to Santiago has been upgraded, otherwise it could mean an unwanted detour. Some might be tempted into this detour to visit the **Centro Alfarero** at Arguayo which is a pottery centre dedicated to ware made by traditional Guanche techniques.

Los Gigantes is a rapidly developing resort which takes its name from the towering black cliffs that form the northern backdrop. Built down a hillside, the road leads towards the marina at the bottom but a road on the right

---

The Pyramids of Güímar

The story of the discovery of the pyramids at Güímar is just as remarkable as the fact that the pyramids exist on the island. Only early in 1990 were the giant heaps of volcanic rocks recognised as pyramids by an amateur enthusiast. His newspaper article was dismissed by local archaeologists but it came to the attention of anthropologistThor Heyerdahl, a world authority.

Heyerdahl was soon convinced of their authenticity and test excavations in 1991 conducted by archaeologists from La Laguna University confirmed the existence of four main step-pyramids. Each pyramid had a carefully constructed stairway on the western face leading to a summit platform from where the rising sun can be viewed. Full excavations took place only in 1997.

Norwegian ship owner Fred aOlsen, long-time friend of Thor Heyerdahl, stepped in to save the pyramids and financed a Culture Park and an international archaeological research foundation. The park is well laid out, allowing visitors to wander around to view the pyramids, and the museum sets out to answer the many questions posed by their existence.

After a lifetime's study of pyramids in various parts of the world, Thor Heyerdahl's explanation of how and why they are there is credible and convincing. A 15-minute video shown in the auditorium explains how the ocean currents sweep down from the north-eastern coast of Africa to Central America, passing the Canary Islands along the way, and how reed boats might have travelled on these currents. With this knowledge, it hardly seems coincidence that step-pyramids, like those here on Tenerife, exist at stations along the way, from Egypt to Central America and Peru.

An exhibition of reed boats and the opportunity to see papyrus in growth, from which the boats are made, rounds off an intriguing and thought-provoking exhibition. Should your visit absorb more time than expected, there are facilities on site including a cafeteria and an excellent *tasca* (tavern) on the road nearby.

Güímar is reached from Playa de las Américas by taking the motorway to Santa Cruz and turning off at the 23km junction to Puerto de Güímar and following signposts inland to Güímar then to the pyramids. The park is open daily 9.30am–6pm, except 25 December. 25th and 1 January. www.piramidesdeguimar.net

just before this is reached leads to the small beach set beneath the cliffs. Scuba diving is popular in these clear waters and, with the marina on hand, there are plenty of boats offering trips. As a resort, it has a different character from any other on the island and manages to attract a faithful band of followers despite the hilly terrain.

Further around this craggy coastline is the fishing village of **Puerto de Santiago** which has also expanded into a popular tourist resort, although the harbour still remains. Hotels and apartments are now very much part of the scene but it has a large and beautiful beach of glistening black sand with attractively laid out-gardens at the southern end.

Banana plantations spread up the hillsides here and dominate the scenery for a time. San Juan, further along the coast, need not detain us since there is little of interest. A loop road descends to the promenade and back up to the main road and a drive around the loop is enough to give a flavour of this fairly busy town which has only a tiny beach. Playa de las Américas is not too far away now.

The Orotava Valley

A day of startling contrasts is in store on this tour. Traverse the lunar landscape of Las Cañadas, then descend through pine woods into the island's most fertile valley to visit the old colonial style town of La Orotava.

Prepare for a good day's driving with stops along the way to admire the views and a couple of hours' stop in Orotava. If time allows, head down into Puerto de la Cruz (see p45) or save it for another day. Return back round the coast via Icod, (see Car Tour 4 Page 65) a slow but scenic journey of around two hours or, if time is of the essence, the longer motorway route via Santa Cruz takes a little over an hour back to Los Cristianos.

Start out by following the route of Car Tour 2 (see p56) from Los Cristianos as far as the Visitor Centre at El Portillo. Continue on to soon reach a road junction. Keep ahead round left here towards La Orotava. Once clear of the trees, Valle de la Orotava (Orotava Valley) spreads like a gently undulating carpet down to the developments which now fringe the coast; a huge shallow, sloping bowl 10km by 11km (6 miles by 7 miles) clinging to the lower skirts of Teide. The Guanches were the first to appreciate its fertile soil and temperate year-round climate and founded a settlement, Araotava, on the site of present day Orotava. Part of the rich Guanche kingdom of Taora, it was taken over and continued to flourish under the Spanish conquerors in the 15th century.

Wealthy foreign visitors began to discover the delights of this region at the end of the 19th century and settled in the area. Their descendants are now being joined by those grown rich on tourism and much land previously farmed is being lost to housing. Those in search of a more rural experience might like to take the high road across the valley, as far as Cruz Santa just before Los Realejos, then back to La Orotava on a lower road. Best of all is to return at another time and walk the many paths

Car Tours

which criss-cross the valley.

First impressions of La Orotava might suggest a modern sprawl but it is well worth a stop. Round to the left of the confluence of roads at the bottom is the Plaza de la Constitución and a good place to start a tour of the old town.

La Orotava

Old Orotava is a closely knit enclave of narrow cobbled streets and 17th-19th century mansions with their Canarian balconies and traditional shuttered windows. Many of its fine old buildings, museums and points of interest are signposted but this tour plots a logical route. Sunday is the best day for parking. To park, follow Teide signs through the town. Pick up 'P San Augistin' signs and stay ahead into a narrow street, as the main road bends left, to a multi-storey car park, but, unfortunately, most of the museums are closed. Head first for the main square.

Superb views over the roofs of the old

La Orotava

town and down to the coast from Plaza de la Constitución have led it to be known as 'the balcony of La Orotava'.

La Orotava

Dominant in a corner of the square sits the Church and Former Monastery of **San Agustín** (St Augustine). An old window adds interest to the façade of the belltower next to which projects a beautifully carved balcony.

Continue along Carrera del Escultor Estévez and turn right down Calle Tomás Zerolo between old mansions to visit the one-time Convento de Santo Domingo which now houses the **Museo de Artesania Iberoamericana** (Museum of Spanish-American Crafts, open 9.30am–6pm Mon–Sat). This extensive collection of musical instruments, strange dolls and figurines, pots and even a reed boat is housed in rooms around the central courtyard. Across the road from Santo Domingo, and run in tandem with the museum, is **Casa Torrehermosa**. This old mansion is the official Empresa Insular de Artesanía (island enterprise craft workshop) which has a selection of crafts for sale.

Returning back uphill, turn first right into Calle Viera then left up Calle Cologán to Plaza Casañas and **Iglesia de Nuestra Señora de la Concepción**, recognisable by its high dome. The present church dates from the 18th century, the original 16th century foundation succumbing to an earthquake in 1705. Considered a fine example of baroque architecture with touches of rococo, the interior decoration is highly regarded with a hint of neoclassical in the Greek rotunda appearance of the cupola above the altar.

The steep Calle Colegio starts behind the church, rises past the large creamy frontage of the House of Leccard to the **Casa de los Balcones** (House of the Balconies) in Calle San Francisco.

Traditional Canarian balconies grace the walls of these early mansions whose patios (inner courtyards), lined with yet more delicately carved balconies, provide an intriguing glimpse of early colonial living. Casa de los Balcones at No. 3 was built in 1632 and is now a museum and an embroidery school, established to conserve the art of drawn thread work (*calados*) and embroidery (*bordellos*). At one time a town or village could be identified by the patterns of its drawn thread work and here can be purchased some of the best examples on the island. Rooms on the upper storey, furnished in 19th century style, provide a fascinating mirror on the past, even down to the kitchen and bathroom. Down in the courtyard, a wine press overlooks the weaving of baskets while inside, the ladies of the embroidery school skilfully apply their needles. The house opposite Casa de los Balcones, **Casa del Turista** (1590), is also a craft centre from whose terrace there are panoramic views out over the valley. A sand painting artist can usually be found at work on a demonstration piece here.

A little further uphill on the right, in Plaza San Francisco, is the **Hospital de la Santísima Trinidad** which started life as a Franciscan convent in 1600. Since 1884 it has served as a hospital for the mentally handicapped. The revolving drum in the main door was used to leave foundling babies anonymously. Views from its accessible terrace are magnificent.

Take Calle Hermano Apolinar, off right at the bottom of Plaza San Francisco, to reach the **Hijuela de Botánico** (Daughter of the Botanic Garden, open

8am–2pm daily except Sunday and holidays). It was planted as a miniature offshoot of the Botanic Garden at Puerto de la Cruz in 1923. Below the garden is the 1871 Palacio Municipal (Town Hall) fronted by the Plaza de General Franco. During the May/June celebrations of Corpus Christi, this square is filled with sand paintings. The paintings, all with a religious theme, are a marvel of artistic endeavour using volcanic sands and ash from Las Cañadas and coloured earth. It seems unbelievable that such effort is destroyed in seconds by the Corpus Christi day procession as it passes over them. A similar celebration in La Laguna uses flower petals to create floral carpets.

Cross the junction of Calle León and Tomás Pérez, opposite the Botanic Garden, and enter the gardens **Marquesado de la Quinta Roja**. This unexpectedly delightful oasis was constructed in the 19th century. The main entrance at the lower end leads directly back into Plaza de la Constitución.

From Orotava head down towards the motorway and an option to visit the **Museo de Cerámica** (Pottery Museum, open daily 10am–6pm with a free bus from Playa Martiánez in Puerto de la Cruz). This is located on the La Luz/Las Candias road, towards Los Realejos, about 2km (1.5 miles) along just past the Tafuriaste development. Housed in the 17th century Casa Tafuriaste, the collection is one of the most complete in Spain. It is a working pottery and the museum provides a fascinating insight into an enormous range of pottery utensils and their uses.

Once back on the main road head towards Icod. Just below Los Realejos keep an eye open for **Mirador Terraza San Pedro** on the right. This lovely viewpoint looks out over banana plantations and along the coast in both directions. Just below is the Ermita de San Pedro, approached along a cobbled trail but the café/restaurant provides a good enough excuse to stop and soak up the coastal ambience.

The Teno Mountains (Macizo de Teno)

Tucked away in the western corner of the island is a range of hills known as Macizo de Teno. Although not even one third of the height of Pico de Teide, the steep-sided valleys and sharp ridges are as dramatic as they are dynamic and their rugged appearance defies all but the fearless. Starting from Santiago del Teide, there is a road through the heart of the mountains which visits the spectacularly situated village of Masca before emerging at Buenavista. Also included in this tour is the lighthouse at Punto de Teno, the ancient port of Garachico and Icod de los Vinos which is famous for its venerable dragon tree.

Pick up the motorway at Playa de los Américas and head northwards. Ignore the coastal route and stay on the road which passes through the important agricultural centre of Guia de Isora. Quick progress is not always possible along these roads. **Santiago del Teide** provides an opportunity for a refreshment stop but, for pleasanter surroundings, it might be advantageous to wait until Masca is reached which is not too far away from here.

The road out to Masca is set to test a few nerves. A corniche road climbs through hairpin bends to cross over a pass but the edges are protected with concrete blocks which lend a feeling of security. There is a pull-off at the top which offers early views of Masca and another a little further on with equally breathtaking views. **Masca** itself sits out on a narrow ridge extending just as far as a huge cone of rock and is accessible only on foot, so leave the car in the parking area provided by the village entrance. The hillsides around Masca are very green and extensively terraced but they seem to have fallen into disuse, suggesting that this hamlet thrives on the whim of a new paymaster: tourism. Part of the village has been spruced up with newly paved walkways, palm trees and a number of the houses converted into tourist shops and cafés. Walking down the neatly paved footpath and out along the ridge gives a different perspective on its location but the return walk reveals another, less prosperous section of the village which can be reached by following the track off to the right. Wandering up the narrow streets between the old houses leads back to the main road just above the car park. There is a very popular walk which sets out from Masca leading down to the sea following the Barranco de Masca. Organised walking parties are picked up by boat.

The onward route to Buenavista teems with more breathtaking views

Teno Lighthouse

of massively terraced hillsides and rugged volcanic hills. **Buenavista** is the largest town in the area and thrives on agriculture. Its spacious town square is dominated by the white church of the Virgen de los Remedios with its tiered belltower and surrounded by handsome 17th and 18th century houses with traditional wooden balconies. Pick up signs for **Punta de Teno** which leads out to a lighthouse at the most westerly point of the island.

There is little activity around the lighthouse these days and the spit of volcanic rock here is mostly frequented by fishermen and day trippers who rarely stay long since there is not much to detain them. Walkways provide good access to the various viewpoints. Watching the waves crash white surf against the rocks can be quite mesmeric and, on a clear day, the islands of La Gomera and La Palma can be seen and, looking south, the sheer cliffs of Los Gigantes can be recognised.

Return by the outward route to Buenavista and continue along the coast road towards Garachico. **Los Silos**, passed en route, seems to have settled for staying outside tourism in spite of earlier plans. Its shady plaza and brilliant white church tempt many to stop and there is a seawater swimming pool for cooling off. The pretty coastal town of **Garachico** is firmly woven into the history of Tenerife but perhaps for the wrong reason. It was founded by the Spanish and developed as the island's main harbour for the wine trade. This was brought to a crashing halt by the eruption of Volcán de Negro in 1706 which poured molten lava down onto the town, destroying the harbour and virtually the whole of the village. Puerto de la Cruz and Santa Cruz took over the task of exporting the wines and even when Garachico was rebuilt, on top of the old lava flow, it was never able to recapture its former importance.

Looked over by Pico de Teide, Garachico remains a thriving village popular with day trippers and tourists. Neatly laid out with crescent streets of white houses which follow the natural curves of the lava peninsula, it has an inviting charm which persuades visitors that this is a place to explore. Down on the seafront there is a complex of natural rock pools created by the cooling effect of the sea on the lava

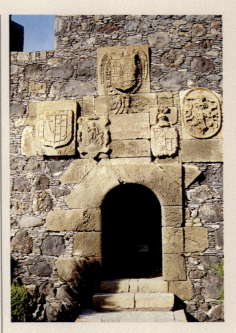

Castillo de San Miguel

from the 1706 volcano. Washed and cleaned by the action of the tides, they are available to swimmers only when the sea is not rough. Nearby here and overlooking the sea is the 16th century **Castillo de San Miguel** which is one of only a few buildings to escape destruction in 1706. It belonged to the Counts of Gomera but it now houses a small museum of rocks and shells. The other significant building which survived is the Convento de San Francisco, now the Casa de Cultura, which holds regular exhibitions. Wandering the streets admiring some of the older style architecture is part of the pleasure of Garachico and inevitably this leads to the town square where stands the 18th century parish church of Santa Ana. The bandstand here is thoughtfully designed with a café bar beneath, typical of bandstands in the north of the island. Those lucky enough to be around on the first Sunday of the month can enjoy a very popular handicraft fair.

If time is running away, this tour can be shortened by taking the road which snakes its way uphill to Tanque and the main road back to Playa de las Américas. There are some terrific bird's eye views back down over Garachico from this road up to Tanque. Those intent on completing the tour should continue on to Icod de los Vinos before returning.

It must be very rare for a tree to become a major tourist attraction but **Icod de los Vinos** boasts a 1,000-year-old dragon tree, *Drago milenario*, which pulls in the crowds daily and there is hardly a tour coach passing this way that does not stop. It is well signposted so there is little problem in driving into the right area but parking might be a different problem.

Estimates of the tree's age vary very considerably with the romantics dreaming of 2–3,000 years while the more down-to-earth botanists count only in hundreds, perhaps three to five. Since this is not really a tree but a member of the Agave family, so the trunk does not form annual rings which are normally used to assess the age of a tree, the age of this one really is down to guesswork. Whatever, it is a truly majestic specimen with a girth of around 6m (20ft) and reaching up like a multi-tentacled hydra to around 17m (56 ft). The tree is actually indigenous to the island and there are plenty around but none of this age. When the tree is cut it bleeds red. Apart from the dragon tree, attention in Icod focuses around the old part for

interesting architecture with more than a few traditional wooden balconies on view and shoppers will be pleased to learn that it has a modern shopping centre good enough to attract locals from far and wide.

From here the C820 leads back to Playa de las Américas, but leave at least two hours since the journey can be quite slow.

The Anaga Peninsula

Located in the area above Santa Cruz, the green-cloaked Anaga peninsula, isolated, rugged and beautiful, offers unrivalled scenery. La Laguna, the island's first capital, is visited at the end of the tour for a little sightseeing and perhaps some shopping. For directness and speed, the autopista is recommended as the route from Playa de las Américas up to Santa Cruz to start the tour. Expect narrow roads on the peninsula which can be slow to drive even though distances are not great. Some are corniche roads perched on the mountainside but these are well protected with concrete blocks for security and should not cause too much anxiety if taken carefully.

On the way north to Santa Cruz it is worth a few minutes to stop at **Candelaria**, the religious centre of the island. There is a legend which tells of how a statue of the Virgin holding a naked child in one arm and a candle in the other was washed up onto the rocks close to Candelaria in the 14th century. It was found by the Guanches and taken to a cave at Achbinico (now San Blas) where it became an object of veneration although they knew nothing about Christianity. That part of the legend is fairly consistent although it does have embellishments. The next part varies considerably but this is one version. Some 70 years later, a young Spanish nobleman stole the statue and took it back to his church in Fuerteventura but when the priest came the next morning, the statue had turned to face the wall. It was turned around but next day it was again facing the wall. A plague broke out on the island so the statue was returned to Candelaria where she became known as Nuestra Señora de la Candelaria and adopted as the patron saint of the Canaries. In 1826 a tidal wave washed the statue out to sea and it was never seen again. The present statue is a copy made a few years later. The Basilica of Candelaria, the home of the statue, dominates the town and is the focus of the huge pilgrimage which takes place annually on 14/15 August. Outside the church is a vast square guarded by stone statues of the Guanche kings.

On reaching Santa Cruz, take the first exit signposted for the port (*puerto*) which leads down to the marginal and, with no decisions for the driver but to continue ahead, is the simplest way to cross the capital to head out to **San Andrés**. Before turning at San Andrés to head up into the mountains of the Anaga Peninsula, just keep ahead for a moment to look at **Playa de las Teresitas**, man-made but easily the most beautiful beach on the island. Back now to the untidy-looking San Andrés and the mountains. The road climbs quickly, following the line of Barranco de las Huertas and providing the spectacle of a fertile valley floor with arid, scrub-covered hillsides. This changes fairly soon for the Anaga peninsula is generally well forested and green. Having wound around a few more corners on nearing the backbone of the peninsula, be prepared to turn right for Taganana. This is a spur road down to the coast and it means returning the same way but the tireless waves of green hills look different from every perspective.

The white houses of **Taganana** defy the steep hillsides. Equally gravity-defying are the farmed terraces covering the hillsides which provide the Tagananians with an excellent wine which is no small compensation, if any were needed, for living in such an isolated and beautiful spot. The road continues along the coast as far as Benijo offering wilderness views of a dark rocky seashore in this forgotten corner of the island. **Roque de las Bodegas**, passed en route, has a small string of fish restaurants which are especially popular with the Tenerifians.

Return through Taganana back to the top of the spine. Intrepid explorers might wish to drive the 10km (6.25 mile) spur out to **Chamorga** but the road on this section is narrow with passing places and only worthwhile if the day is fine since the clouds readily build and roll over this crest eliminating its best asset, the views. Instead turn through the laurel and tree heather towards La Laguna. Two stops lie ahead. First of these is a brief excursion into the valley to visit the small hamlet of **Roques Negro** which is centred, as usual, around a church. The next excursion from the main ridge road is down towards the villages of Las Caboneras

Anaga Peninsula

and Taborno. As you drop down into this steep valley on the northern flank, the road divides to serve these two villages which face each other across the valley, beneath the shadow of the towering peak of Roque de Taborno. **Taborno** is a tiny village of white houses with an equally tiny white church but it does have a bar where the local wine can be tasted. There is some excellent walking in the area and it could start along the footpath which connects Taborno to Las Carbonense (the Charcoal Burners). From there a footpath leads out to the village of **Chinamada** where people live in cave houses cut into the rock, although they do have electricity and some modern conveniences.

Once back on the main road watch

La Laguna; cathedral

out for the junction on the left leading to **Mirador del Pico del Inglés** (Peak of the English) which many claim is the finest viewpoint on the island. Just a little further on is **Mirador Ermita Cruz del Carmen** which is a popular stopping place with a visitor centre and a large picnic area. The centre has an exhibition explaining the island's volcanic history related to the flora and fauna with explanations in English.

From here the road starts to lead off the peninsula down towards La Laguna and a further viewpoint, Mirador de Aguere, shows the verdant plateau which **La Laguna** has made its own. Parking in La Laguna is not always easy but head for the towers of the cathedral and park when possible. Tenerife's first capital and the oldest Spanish town on the island, **San Cristóbal de la Laguna** was founded by Fernández de Lugo in 1496 after he had conquered the island. Originally, it was located by a small lake (*laguna*) but this has long since dried up. It is the most important town on the island next to Santa Cruz and has the distinction of having the only university in the Canaries.

Santa Iglesia, the cathedral, is a good place to start a tour on foot. Founded originally in 1515, it has undergone a number of transformations before the present, rather stern neoclassical structure emerged in 1904. Although a bit cavernous inside, it has its share of treasures but look behind the High Altar for the simple tomb of Fernández de Lugo (1575–1632). Those interested in churches could head right up Calle Obispo Rey Redondo to **Nuestra Señora de la Concepción** which, built in 1502, has the distinction of being the oldest church on the island, but otherwise head left down this same street into Plaza del Adelantado. Houses of character are quite a feature in this square and there are some attractive carved wooden balconies. On the entry corner is the 19th century neoclassical Town Hall (*Ayuntiamento*) while around to the left is the Convent of Santa Catalina and on the opposite side of the road is Palace de Nava, an old colonial baroque mansion. Also in this square is the well-placed Hotel Nivaria and the market hall.

Tenerife History Museum (open 10am–5pm, Sunday 10am–2pm, closed Monday), located at Calle San Agustin, 22, is a fairly new museum located in a magnificent 16th century house and well worth a visit. It provides a good insight into the island's history and economy over the past 500 years and the house too has a courtyard full of wooden balconies and cascading greenery. This street has many stately homes and fine buildings including La Laguna's first university, **Universidad de San Fernando**, with its elegant inner courtyard. La Laguna is worth more than one visit so next time try Sunday morning when the lively market is in full swing.

Getting There

By Air

The easiest way is by charter flight directly from a regional airport in the UK to Reina Sofia airport in the south of the island. Most of the leading tour operators offer both flights and holidays all year round.

Scheduled flights connect Tenerife to the UK–Monarch Airlines (www.flymonarch.com).

Tenerife has two main airports. Reina Sofia in the south is the major airport for international flights while Los Rodeos in the north is used for inter-island flights and some international flights.

By Sea

Visitors from Europe planning to take their own car will need to head first for Cádiz on the Spanish mainland to catch the weekly ferry over to Tenerife. Since there are also ferry services between the islands, it is possible to move on to other islands in the group.

For information and timetables for inter-island ferries, see: www.fredolsen.es

Accommodation

The majority of accommodation on Tenerife, particularly in the south of the island, is relatively recent and has been constructed expressly for package holidaymakers. Independent travellers are most likely to fare better for choice in and around Santa Cruz or Puerto de la Cruz but even here availability is tight over the Christmas period, for Carnival in February/March and over the main summer months. Contact the Spanish National Tourist Office for accommodation lists or check on the internet searching under Tenerife.

Hotels

All hotels and *hostales* are government controlled and prices should be displayed in the reception area. Unless otherwise stated, the prices are for two sharing a double room. Check whether or not breakfast is included and whether prices are inclusive of IGIC, a service tax.

They are classified from one to five stars, according to services and facilities offered. As with most countries, these classifications give little indication as to actual levels of cleanliness or quality of service and fixtures and fittings.

Paradores

There is only one parador on Tenerife, the Cañadas del Teide, a welcoming chalet-type building handy for the cable car (*el teleférico*) which hastens access to the summit of Mount Teide.

For further information and reservations:
☎ 923 38 64 15
fax 923 38 23 52
email: canadas@parador.es

Hostales are a more modest type of hotel and are only rated from one to three stars.
Casas de huéspedes or *pensiones* (guest houses) are usually family-run. These vary from the relatively simple to the luxurious where meals are often an option.

Apartments

By far the most common form of accommodation on Tenerife, apartments come in all guises and sizes from basic through to those containing every conceivable luxury. Most are in purpose-built apartment blocks with swimming pools, and sometimes a restaurant and supermarket. *Hotelapartamentos* or *Aparthotels* are self-catering apartments under the umbrella of a hotel with attendant hotel facilities.

Rural Tourism (Turismo Rural)

In a bid to spread tourism away from the coastal areas to inland local communities, traditional houses are being renovated and made available to rent. These can vary from small village houses to manor houses to small hotels but all are well appointed internally, some offer B&B whilst others are self-catering.

Reservations through ATTUR
☎/Fax 922 230 926
email: jritter@teleline.es

or AECAN
☎ 922 240 816
fax 922 244 003
email: aecan@cip.es
www.cip.es/aecan

Car Hire

A current driving licence is all that is required for EU nationals and others should have an International Driving Permit to be on the safe side. Hirers must be over 21, in some cases 25, and may also be asked for a photocopy of the key identification page of their passport. Check with the hire company if it is intended to take the vehicle on ferries to other islands. Tenerife is relatively inexpensive for car hire but a better deal can often be arranged by booking and paying in advance of departure, not necessarily through a tour company but through the many companies which offer very competitive rates and include full insurance and unlimited mileage. Shop around. These companies operate through an agent on the island and offer rates which can be significantly lower than those available from the agent on the spot. At some high-peak times there could be difficulty in hiring a car once on the island.

There is no shortage of car-hire companies on the island but advertised car rates are very often the basic rate, maybe inclusive of third party insurance, but exclusive of CDW, unlimited mileage, local taxes and a daily insurance rate per occupant. Third party insurance is compulsory under Spanish law and this cost will be added to the basic hire charge. It is imperative to take out Collision Damage Waiver (CDW). Should you be unfortunate enough to be involved in an accident without CDW insurance and the costs cannot be recovered from a third party then the consequences can be frightening. At best you may be faced with a huge repair bill; at worst you could be detained until it is fully paid.

Regular hirers abroad should consider taking out full cover for excess charges. See www.insurance4carhire.co.uk.

Tyres and damage to the underside of the car are mostly excluded from the insurance cover. Take time when you are accepting the car to inspect the tyres and, if not fully satisfied, do not accept the vehicle. Any existing damage to the vehicle and petrol level (if below full) should be recorded before accepting the rental agreement. Be sure to have the telephone number of the agency to hand and contact them first in case of a breakdown. Never call a recovery truck (*grua*) yourself or you'll be liable for the bill.

Under Spanish law, all drivers are obliged to carry their driving licence with them. Also carry your passport and the vehicle hire documents. There are occasional police checks when these will be required to be produced.

Motorcycles

The above comments on insurance apply also to hiring a motorcycle or moped. There is a problem over crash helmets too. The law says very clearly that these must be worn and reputable hire companies provide them with the bike.

Under Spanish law, all drivers are obliged to carry their driving licence with them. Also carry your passport and the vehicle hire documents. There are occasional police checks when these will be required to be produced.

Check the local insurance cover on bikes as theft is often excluded on policies. The onus is on you to be adequately insured or at least securely shackle the bike whenever it is left and be prepared to accept responsibility for any loss.

See also Driving on Tenerife (p78).

Changing Money

Banks are plentiful in main areas of tourism and there are also Exchange Bureaux, located by the 'Cambio' sign. The only problem, sometimes, when changing bank notes or Traveller's Cheques is bureaucracy and you may need your passport for identification purposes.

Credit and cash cards can be used to access cash from ATMs which is by far the easiest and most convenient way of obtaining money. Look for the symbols displayed on the ATM to see if one corresponds to your card. Users can select instructions in English or the language of their choice.

Banks are open weekdays from 9am–2pm and from 9am–12noon on Saturdays but are closed on Saturday during the summer between 1 June and 31 October. Main Post Offices are open weekdays from 9am–2pm and from 9am–12noon or 1pm on Saturday. Banks and Post Offices are closed Sunday and Holidays and cease to exchange currency half an hour before closing time.

Complaints

All hotels, restaurants, campsites and petrol stations are required by law to keep and produce a complaint book/form on request. Ask for *'libro de reclamaciones'*.

Consulates

There are British and Irish consulates on Tenerife but embassies are located on mainland Spain in Madrid.

Nearest Consulates are:

Ireland
La Marina 7
Ed. Hamilton 6th floor
Santa Cruz
Tenerife
☎ 245671

UK
Plaza de Weyler 8
1st floor
Santa Cruz
Tenerife
☎ 286863
(British Embassy in Madrid
☎ 91 319 0200)

USA
contact the American Embassy in Madrid at Calle Serrano 75
28006 Madrid
☎ (91) 587 2303

Crime and Theft

Although crime is on the increase it is usually confined to theft from cars, pickpockets and bag-snatching. Should you be the victim of theft or careless loss, inform the Tourist Police who will issue you with a statement. This document is necessary when claiming from your insurance company. Hotel reception or your holiday representative should be able to help you with this procedure.

If your loss includes a passport then you will need to contact your Consulate/Embassy (see above).

Currency and Credit Cards

Tenerife, as part of Spain, was amongst the first twelve countries to replace their own national currency with the euro. Notes of legal tender have values of 500, 200, 100, 50, 20, 10 and 5 euros. One and two euro coins are available along with 50, 20,10, 5, 2 and 1 cent coins. The notes are identical in design in all countries of the eurozone but the coins have a national design on one side.

Credit cards are acceptable and widely used. Report all lost or stolen cards immediately.

☎ 915 720 303 for American Express, Mastercard and Visa.

Disabled Facilities

In general, facilities for the disabled are extremely limited but the problem is slowly being addressed in more recent building projects. Wheelchairs are available at the airport and many hotels in Playa de las Américas, Los Cristianos and some in Puerto de la Cruz. Always check out exactly what is on offer before booking a particular hotel.

Los Cristianos is particularly wheelchair–friendly with plenty of ramps and a long promenade linking it to Playa de las Américas.

For wheelchair hire and information on suitable accommodation contact:

Orange Badge Wheelchair Hire
☎ 922 797 355
www.orangebadge.com

Le Ro
Edificio Mar y Sol
38650 Los Cristianos
☎ 922 750 289
www.lero.net
Specialises in nursing care and providing or repairing appliances for the disabled.

Active Mobility
☎ 922 789 707
www.activemobility-tenerife.com
Wheelchair and scooter hire.

Driving on Tenerife

Driving on Tenerife is on the right-hand side of the road and overtaking on the left. The wearing of seat belts is compulsory and non-compliance in this respect can result in an on-the-spot fine. Children under 10 must sit in the back of the car.

Unless there are signs indicating otherwise, the speed limits are as follows: built-up areas 50kph (31mph) with variations at 40kph (25mph) or 60kph (37mph); other roads 90kph (56mph); dual carriageways 100kph (62mph) with the motorway (autopista) at 120kph (75mph). Speed limits are rigorously enforced, with on-the-spot fines, and there is little or no leeway allowed.

Random breath testing is in force so do not drink and drive. The limit is the same as that in Britain (80mg) and the consequences of prosecution likewise. Always carry your driving licence (*permiso de conducir*), car hire documents and passport (*el pasaporte*) with you. Failure to produce these on request if stopped will result in an on-the-spot fine. Always ask for a receipt when paying an on-the-spot fine.

Unleaded petrol (*sin plomo*) is freely available. Grades of petrol (*gasolina*) normally on offer are unleaded, Super (4*) and Diesel (*gasóleo* or *gasoil*). Some petrol stations close on Sunday and public holidays.

Blue markings indicate a pay and display area so be sure to obtain a ticket from the machine to leave on the dashboard. These blue zones are operational between the hours of 9am–1.30pm or 2pm and from 4pm or 4.30pm–8pm, except Saturday afternoon, Sunday and official holidays. One exception to watch out for is in Adeje, where a ticket is required at all times. A blue envelope stuck behind a wiper means you have overstayed your paid time and have had the misfortune to be caught by a traffic warden. Fines can be paid by returning to the ticket machine: press the 'Anulación de denuncia' button, insert the correct amount of currency to receive another ticket which is placed with the fine in the box below the machine.

Pedestrians have right of way on zebra crossings, but do not rely on all traffic stopping immediately even for the green man signal.

Road signs and markings are similar to those encountered in the UK but some of the road systems can confuse. Motorway exit numbers are shown in white and the blue number is the kilometre distance from Santa Cruz. A 'Cambio de Sentido' sign meaning literally 'change of mind' is an indication that you can leave the motorway and rejoin the return carriageway.

Duty-free Allowances

Tenerife is Spanish and as such enjoys the benefits of EU membership whereby it receives grants and subsidies. The main difference lies in its duty-free status, a concession it has enjoyed since 1852. Adult EU nationals travelling between member states are allowed to take home one litre of spirits etc. bought duty free at the airport or in flight, in addition to any goods bought duty-paid in the shops. Since goods bought in shops on Tenerife are all duty-free the limited allowance only applies as below.

One litre of Spirits OR Two litres of Sparkling Wine

PLUS

Two bottles of (still) Table Wine

200 Cigarettes OR 50 Cigars OR 250 grams of Tobacco

60ml of Perfume OR 250ml of Toilet Water

Gifts to the value of £145

On leaving the airport pass through the Green or Red customs channel, not the Blue channel normally used when entering from another EU country.

Electricity

Mains electricity is supplied at 220 volts AC. Electrical equipment should be fitted with a continental two-pin plug or an appropriate adapter used. Power cuts are not unknown so a torch could prove useful.

Emergency Telephone Numbers

The telephone number for any emergency is ☎ 112

National Police ☎ 091

Local Police ☎ 092

24-Hour Emergency Medical Services

Las Americas Salud Medical Centre ☎ 922 791 253

Ambulances (Cruz Roja) ☎ 061

Doctor on ☎ 900 112 111 (freephone)

Should you need treatment in hospital or at a clinic you will be required to produce your passport, travel insurance details and your airline ticket.

Fact File

Do not forget to obtain receipts for all medical expenses incurred. Not all travel insurance companies settle accounts directly and the onus may be on you to pay for any treatment and medication required then claiming these costs back from the insurance company.

Health Care

For minor ailments like headaches, mosquito bites or tummy upsets, head for the chemist's shop (*farmacia*), identified by a green cross. On the whole, insects (including mosquitoes) are less of a problem on Tenerife compared with many Mediterranean resorts, especially in the arid south of the island. If you need a further supply of prescription drugs make sure you take a copy of your prescription. Chemists are open from 9am –1pm & 4pm–8pm weekdays and Saturdays 9am–1pm. Duty chemists '*farmacia de guardia*', provide a 24-hour service outside normal working hours. Details of the duty chemist for an area are posted in chemist shop windows, in local papers or by ☎ 922 282 424. Night-time service is for emergency only.

There is no shortage of English-speaking doctors and dentists on the island. Most of these are listed in the widely available selection of local English-language newspapers and magazines. First Aid and treatment centres (*Centro Sanitario*) are dotted around the island and there are major hospitals in Los Cristianos, La Orotava, Playa de las Américas and Santa Cruz, which offer a very high standard of care. Those in search of a dental surgeon should look for an *Estomatologista* or an *Odontólogo* as a *Dentista* is only consulted for the simplest of dental treatment.

Treatment is free under the EC Regulations for those with an EHIC (European Health Insurance Card) but only from doctors practising under the Spanish health care system. In an emergency say you have an EHIC and wish to be treated under the EC arrangements. Besides showing the original EHIC a photocopy will be required each time treatment is needed. You will have to pay up to 40% of the cost of medicines unless an old-age pensioner. To save a great deal of bureaucratic wrangling it is much better to take out adequate holiday insurance cover. Dental treatment will have to be paid for in full and will not be reimbursed.

International Dialling Codes

Codes from Tenerife are as follows:

UK and Northern Ireland 0044 (reverse charge calls via English operator ☎ 900 99 0044)

United States and Canada 001

See also Telephone Services, p92

Lost Property

This should be reported to the Municipal Police or Guardia Civil within 24 hours to obtain an official report which your insurance company will require.

Mosquitoes

As surface water is virtually non-existent on Tenerife, mosquitoes are deprived of a prime breeding ground. If they are encountered, it is more likely to be in the greener north than the dry and arid south of the island and then only in the heat of summer. This is a minor problem but it pays to be prepared. Have to hand insect repellent and antihistamine cream such as Anthisan, which is particularly effective if applied to bites immediately. For the hotel room, an electric machine which slowly vaporises a pellet is very effective, especially with the windows closed, and there are sprays available for more instant results if intruders are spotted.

Museums

There is normally a charge for admission and, apart from some private museums, they are closed on Monday and public holidays.

National Tourist Office

Tourist information offices on Tenerife can be found in all the major resorts. The main ones are listed below.

Santa Cruz
in Plaza de España
☎ 922 239 592
Open 8am–6pm

Puerto de la Cruz
Plaza de la Iglesia (near the main church)
☎ 922 386 000
Open 9am–7pm

Playa de la Arena
Centro Comercial Seguro del Sol
(opp. beach)
☎ 922 110 348
Open 9am–6pm

Playa de las Américas
Urbanización Torviscas
(opp. Hotel la Pinta)
☎ 922 750 633
Open 9am–4pm
Also in the centre
☎ 922 797 668
Open 9am–1pm & 4–7pm

Las Galletas
Avenida Marítima
☎ 922 730 133
Open 9am–1pm & 4–7pm

Los Cristianos
Las Vistas
☎ 922 787 011
Open 9am–1pm & 4–7pm

Nightlife

Choices are wide-ranging and there is something to suit everybody. Candlelit dinners through to an al fresco moonlit barbecue on the beach will appeal to the romantics while others are drawn by the pulsating beat of all-night discos.

Most hotels have cabaret nights and a range of nightclubs offer exotic floorshows while casinos are on hand for those in search of a sophisticated 'flutter'.

Casinos

A visit to one of Tenerife's three casinos provides a good excuse to dress up. Smart dress and your passport are a requirement of entry. Take your choice from Casino Taoro in Puerto de la Cruz, Casino Playa de las Américas (by Hotel Gran Tinerfe) and Casino Santa Cruz (beneath Hotel Mencey off Rambla General Franco).

Nightclubs

Of the selection of nightclubs the subterranean Andromeda, on an island in the Martiánez complex at Puerto de la Cruz, is highly regarded or, for something different, try Castillo at San Miguel which hosts a Medieval Show.

Discotheques

Playa de las Américas is the hub of discoland in southern Tenerife with Puerto de la Cruz a less frenetic northern counterpart. Indoor and outdoor discos abound but be aware that the press of discos and pubs in the area of Verónicas, in Playa de las Américas, is a known trouble spot.

Nudism

Topless bathing is commonplace on all public beaches and around hotel swimming pools on Tenerife. Nude bathing is not generally acceptable on public beaches but is practised on some of the more remote and secluded beaches.

Police

Policing comes under three separate departments; The Policia Municipal (blue uniform) deal with traffic and cover general policing in towns; the Policia National (brown uniform) deal with crime in towns and the Guardia Civil (green uniform) patrol roads and deal with crime in rural areas.

Postal Services

Post Offices (*Correos*) open on weekdays from 9am–2pm and 9am–1pm on Saturday. Queues for stamps (*sellos*) in busy resorts can be slow but they can be bought along with the cards, at hotel reception or at tobacconists. (Stamps bought in places other than a post office might incur a small surcharge.)

Post in the yellow boxes which sometimes have two slots, one for España and the other marked *extranjeros* (foreign).

Postcards are regarded as low priority and invariably arrive home after your return.

Public Holidays and Festivals

The Tenerifian calendar overflows with red letter days; public holidays, Saints' days and festivals. On public holidays, banks, shops (except maybe souvenir shops in tourist areas) and offices are closed although restaurants normally stay open. Public transport is often interrupted too, reverting to either a Sunday service or to none at all. Petrol stations also close for many of the holidays. The days to watch out for are:

1 January – New Year's Day (Año Nuevo)

6 January – Epiphany

2 February – Candlemas (in Candelaria)

Maundy Thursday & Good Friday

19 March – St Joseph's Day

1 May – Labour Day (Día del Trabajo)

30 May – Canary Day

May/June – Corpus Christi

25 July – St James's Day (Santiago Apóstol, Spain's patron saint)

15 August – Assumption (Asunción)

12 October – Discovery of America (Día de la Hispanidad)

1 November – All Saints' Day (Todos los Santos)

6 December – Constitution Day

8 December – Immaculate Conception (Immaculada Concepción)

25 December – Christmas Day

There are many local fiestas, the best known being *Carnaval* (Carnival) which lasts for three weeks leading up to Lent, and summer *romeriás* (religious festivals) get under way when the eight days of Corpus Christi end in June. Two of the best known of these take place in La Orotava and La Laguna where the spectacular effect of carpets of flowers and sand paintings draw the crowds.

The Spanish equivalent of our April Fool's Day takes place on 28 December, the Day of the Holy Innocents (Día de los Inocentes).

Public Toilets

These can be found in shopping centres, at bus stations and behind some beaches. Toilets in café/bars, restaurants and hotels provide another option as well as providing an excuse to stop for refreshments. You do not have to be a customer but it is polite to ask first.

Terms for toilets are the usual WC, *servicios* or *aseos* while doors are usually marked Señoras or Damas (ladies) and Señores, Caballeros or Hombres (gentlemen).

Public Transport

Buses

The green livery of the TITSA bus service is a common sight on the island and most of the buses are new and air-conditioned. They are reliable, cover an extensive network of routes and offer express services (*directo*) between the main resorts and the capital along the autopista (motorway). Buses on Tenerife are known as *guaguas* (wahwahs); a linguistic throwback. Maps and timetables are available from main bus stations in Avenida Tres de Mayo, Santa Cruz; Playa de las Américas and Puerto de la Cruz. Timetables are also posted at main bus terminals and are available at tourist information posts. As a precaution, always check return times with the driver if going to more out-of-the-way destinations, especially on Sunday and holidays.

Ferries

Ferry services connect all the islands and there is a speedy hydrofoil or jetfoil service between Tenerife (Los Cristianos) and La Gomera (San Sebastian). Further details and timetables can be obtained from the local tourist office.

Taxis

Taxis have a green light on the roof which shows when they are available for hire and must have an official plate with the letters SP (*servicio público*). Drivers should carry an approved list of fares between the major towns and from the airport which you can ask to see. Taxis do have meters but these seem to be rarely used outside Santa Cruz. A reasonable fixed fare structure seems to operate successfully within or between resorts which is usually honestly applied. The going rates are common knowledge–ask at the tourist office–but taxi drivers are permitted to add surcharges at night, weekends and on public holidays. The best policy is to agree a

Fact File

price prior to undertaking a journey.

Taxis can also be used for trips to sights of interest around the island and costs can be reasonable, especially if four are sharing. Enquire at taxi ranks.

Shopping

Normal opening hours are 9am–1pm and 4pm or 5pm –7pm or 9pm with half-day closing on Saturday. Some tourist shops, large supermarkets and stores will remain open during 'siesta' hours between 1–4pm and at weekends. At the height of the season, shopping hours in the resorts are usually extended.

Although the Canaries have been a 'duty-free' zone since 1852, not all the benefits are passed on to the customer. Signs such as 'duty-free' or 'tax-free' can be misleading and are often used as enticements, but the goods may not necessarily be the bargains suggested. Wines, spirits and tobacco though are an exception and significantly cheaper in local shops than in the Airport 'duty-free'. Goods are subject to a local tax (IGIC) of 4%.

The best shopping used to be in Santa Cruz or Puerto de la Cruz but new shopping centres in the Costa Adeje area offer some good alternatives. Traditional wares can be found in craft workshops (_centros artesanias_) in various locations around the island. These include hand-embroidered tablecloths and place mats etc. (calados), lace work similar to Venetian lace from Vilaflor, leather goods, basketry made from palm leaves, pottery and wood carvings but, although these authentic goods are superior in quality, they face stiff competition from the flood of cheap imports found in most shops and markets. Spanish gold is not hallmarked so is less valuable.

Markets

Traditional and more local markets are found mainly in the north of the island where most of the indigenous population lives. These are the places to find local colour and buy fresh fruit, vegetables, fish, meat, cheese and flowers at local prices. Opening hours are normally 9am-1pm Monday to Saturday.

Santa Cruz market

Mercado de Nuestra Señora de Africa (Market of Our Lady of Africa). This is the major market on the island.

La Laguna
La Laguna in Plaza del Adelantado.
Sunday 9am–12noon in the Plaza de Cristo.
A local market selling everything, including animals.

Puerto de la Cruz
Avenida de Blas Pérez González.

Tourist markets are what their title implies. Go there to look at clothing or choose souvenirs by all means but do not expect to find genuine local colour.

Garachico Handicrafts Fair
On the first Sunday of the month. In summer held on the waterfront and in winter outside the San Franciscan Convent next to the Town Hall.

Hippy Market
Every night in Playa de las Américas, near Hotel Park Troya.

Los Cristianos
Every Sunday morning (near the Arona Gran Hotel).

Puerto de la Cruz
Municipal Market with around 200 stalls. 10am–5pm every Wednesday, Friday & Sunday. Centrally located at San Felipe/El Tejar near to Hotel Florida.

Santa Cruz
9am–1pm Sunday Market (El Rastro). Held in the area around Mercado Nuestra Señora de Africa. Sells just about everything.

Torviscas Market
Costa Adeje on Calle de Bruselas, opposite El Duque Commercial Centre, 9am–3pm Thursday and Saturday.

Vilaflor-Mercadillos
9am–4pm Sunday. Billed as the tourist market in the mountains. Market day may vary due to the weather or season.

Sports and Pastimes

Tenerife is a windsurfers' delight and followers flock to the many centres concentrated in the south of the island. Plenty of other water sports are on offer but, on windy days, participation is often at the whim of the Atlantic rollers. Golf, horse riding, tennis and walking are some of the other many and varied pursuits available away from the beach.

For detailed information visit www.abcanarias.com, click on Tenerife and then on Leisure and Sports .

Afternoon Tea Dance

The Columbus Hotel Ballroom

Playa de las Americas

☎ 661 370 800

www.tenerifeteadance.com

Mon–Thur 2pm–5pm.

Bowls

British Games Club Puerto de la Cruz

(opposite Hotel Parque San Antonio).

Doctor Bowls, Parque Loros Las Américas, Playa de las Américas. Floodlit bowls; daily competitions.

The Sporting Club; Wimpey Leisure's Sporting Club, Los Gigantes. Synthetic outdoor bowling greens.

Go-karting

Karting Club Tenerife, Carretera del Cho (on road between Guaza and Las Chafiras which runs parallel and to the south of the motorway between junctions 25 & 26), ☎ 922 730 703. Open daily from 10am. Junior, formula and competition karts are available for hire. Free bus from Los Cristianos and Playa de las Américas.

Karting Las Américas, Carretera General del Sur, Adeje.

☎ 922 710 096.

Off main road from Playa de las Américas to Los Gigantes at Fañabe. Open daily 9am–9pm. Free bus from Los Cristianos and Playa de las Américas.

Golf

There are at present nine established golf courses on Tenerife with more planned. See www.webtenerife.com for more details.

Horse riding

The majority of horse riding establishments, some for club members only, are located in the north of the island, but there is a centre close to the main resort areas in the south.

El Rodeo de la Paja
Caminola Villa, El Ortigal (between La Laguna and Esperanza)
☎ 922 254 011
Lessons are given in an indoor arena but instruction is in Spanish.

Amarilla Golf and Country Club
Costa del Silencio
☎ 922 730 319
Horse riding available to non-members.

Quad Biking

Off-road adventure Quad Park
14yrs plus
☎ 922 725 176/636 333 948
www.thequadparktenerife.com

Safaris

Make your choice of transport here from camel, donkey or jeep.

Camel & Donkey (Burros) Rides & Treks
Camel rides and Donkey Safaris are always a big attraction at El Tanque, near Garachico and Camels at Camel Park near Chayofa, Los Cristianos,
☎ 922 721 080

Jeep Safaris
enquire locally

Submarine Safari
At San Miguel Marina
Amarill Golf.
Costa del Silencio
☎ 922 736 629
www.submarinesafaris.com

Walking

There are walking opportunities on the island but pay attention to weather conditions and footwear. The terrain can be particularly stony. Guided walks are the most suitable for inexperienced walkers or walks which are easy to follow, like the Barranco del Infierno walk above Adeje. (see p57).

The best walking guides are Noel Rochford's *Landscapes of Tenerife* and *Landscapes of Southern Tenerife and La Gomera* (published by Sunflower Books, London), which are also available on the island.

The bookshop at Puerto Colon (facing inland) sells maps and walking books.

Guided walks in the Cañadas National Park, with an interpreter, leave from the Visitor centre (Centro de Visitantes), El Portillo. ☎ 922 259 903/256 440, weekdays only at 9.30am, 11.30am and 1.30pm. Make sure of a place by telephoning ahead. The walks are organised by ICONA, the Spanish nature conservancy organisation, who provide leaflets and maps showing footpaths, available from ICONA and tourist offices. ICONA, Santa Cruz office, ☎ 922 290 129/290 183.

A number of companies are now offering guided walking tours on a daily basis.

Water Sports

There are plenty of opportunities to indulge in a whole range of water sports. For diving, fishing, sailing, scuba diving and boat excursions see the website: www.abcanarias.com/Tenerife: click on Leisure and Sports.

Reputable centres have their own insurance but check your medical insurance cover for let-out clauses, should you suffer injury.

Jet-skiing

Achieving speeds up to 60mph (100kph), a jet-ski can be lethal in the hands of the inexperienced so this sport is now carefully controlled and regulated. Special areas are set aside. On a cautionary note, be aware that responsibility of damage to persons, property and the machine itself is likely to fall firmly on the hirer.

Jet Ski Yamaha (opposite Palm Beach Club) and Puerto Colón, Playa de las Américas.

Surfing

Surfing is available in many parts but Playa Martiánez at Puerto de la Cruz is one of the best locations. Beware of rough seas and dangerous currents.

Underwater Scooter

Ride a scooter underwater. Based at Puerto Colon. Minimum height 1.55m (5ft 4in).

☎ 670 839 516

www.bob-diving.com

Fact File

Water-skiing

Playa de las Américas

Windsurfing

A popular sport on many beaches but the main centres are at El Médano and Playa de las Américas, opposite the Palm Beach Club.

Sunbathing

Year-round sun is one of Tenerife's main attractions but bear in mind that the island lies off the coast of Africa and is nearer the equator than European resorts. In this part of the world, a combination of a clear atmosphere and more direct sun is very burning. Even cloud cover offers little protection. Sunburn and sunstroke can easily spoil your holiday and considerable care needs to be exercised, especially in the early days. Great care is needed in protecting yourself and high factor sun creams should be used. Avoid, if possible, sunbathing in the middle of the day, from 10am to around 2pm when the sun is at its highest and most direct. Suncreams help considerably but, at least for the first few days, take some very light clothing to cover up and control the exposure of your skin to the sun. A slowly acquired tan lasts longer.

Even mild sunburn can be painful and may cause a chill feeling but if fever, vomiting or blistering occur then professional help is essential.

Swimming

There are days when the sea is too rough for all but very strong swimmers. Bathers are strongly advised to respect the flag warning system (see p33). Make sure you choose accommodation with, or with access to, a pool and there are lidos at Santa Cruz and Puerto de la Cruz. See also Beach Guide p33.

Telephone Services & Internet

Hotels usually offer a telephone service, often from the room, but expect to pay a premium for the convenience.

There are modern telephone booths on the island and these take phonecards. Calls within the island do not need an area code but for an international line dial the country code and number required minus the initial 0 (see International Dialing Codes p81).

Calls are cheaper after 10pm weekdays, 2pm Saturday and all day Sunday.

Most large hotels provide an internet service at a price. There are internet cafés around but you have to look for them.

Tenerife Time

Tenerife is in line with the UK and works on GMT. Like the UK it advances its clock one hour in spring, at the end of March, and returns to GMT at the end of autumn. The Canary Islands remain one hour behind the rest of Spain throughout the year.

Tipping

A tip of around 10% is normal for taxi drivers and restaurants who offer good service but many hotels and restaurants include a service charge on the bill (*la cuenta*). Tip the maid at your hotel on leaving and nominal amounts are also appreciated by porters who carry your baggage.

Tourist Offices

Spanish National Tourist Offices

Information on Tenerife and the Canary Islands can be obtained before departure from the Spanish National Tourist Office, addresses as follows:

United Kingdom

22–23 Manchester Square
London W1U 3PX
☎ 020 7486 8077

USA

Water Tower Place
845 North Michigan Avenue
Chicago, IL 606121
☎ (1312) 642 1992

8383 Wilshire Blvd
Suite 960, Beverly Hills
Los Angeles, CA 90211
☎ (1213) 658 7188

1221 Brickell Avenue
Miami, FL 33131
☎ (1305) 358 1992

666 Fifth Avenue 35th
New York, NY 10103
☎ (1212) 265 8822

Canada

2 Bloor Street West
34th Floor, Toronto,
Ont. M4W 3E2
☎ (1416) 961 3131

Water

The water on Tenerife is fine for cleaning teeth but swings between tasting highly chlorinated or vaguely salty, which does not make it good to drink. Quality varies around the island but use only bottled water for drinking and maybe even for making tea and coffee. Five-itre containers of the cheapest brand are fine for normal use. Mineral water (*água mineral*), usually served in cafés/restaurants, comes either *sin gas* (still) or *con gas* (fizzy).

Index

A

Anaga Peninsula	68
Anaga peninsula	68
Apartments	73
Aquapark	23,40
Arona	58

B

Bananera El Guanche	45
Barranco del Infierno	57
botanical garden	45
Bowls	88
Buenavista	66

C

Camello	47
Camel Park	40
Candelaria	68
Capilla San Telmo	48
Casa de la Real Aduana	48
Casa de los Balcones	64
Casa del Turista	64
Casa del Vino la Baranda	47
Casa Iriarte	49
Casa Torrehermosa	64
Casinos	82
Castillo de San Felipe	48
Castillo de San Miguel	67
Centro Alfarero	60
Chamorga	69
Chinamada	70
church of Nuestra Señora de la Peña de Francia	49
Church of the Assumption	39
Climate	16
Costa Adeje	32
Costa del Silencio	32

D

Discotheques	82
Dragon Tree	10

E

El Médano	31,36,56
El Portillo	60
Exotic Park	40

G

Garachico	67
Go-karting	88
Golf	88
Good Beach Guide	33

H

Hijuela de Botánico	64
Horse riding	89
Hospital de la Santísima Trinidad	64
Hotels	72

I

Icod de los Vinos	68
Iglesia de Nuestra Señora de la Concepción	64

J

Jet-skiing	90

L

La Casa de los Balcones	52
La Gomera	39
La Laguna	71
La Laguna Grande	41
La Orotava	63
Las Cañadas del Teide	56
Las Galletas	55
Lido Martiánez	47
Loro Parque	41,47

Los Abrigos	56
Los Cristianos	32,36
Los Gigantes	33,61
Los Realejos	37
Los Roques de García	60
Los Silos	67

M

Macizo de Teno	65
Marquesado de la Quinta Roja	65
Martiánez Lido	48
Masca	55,65
Mercado de Nuestra Señora de Africa	52
Mirador del Pico del Inglés	71
Mirador Ermita Cruz del Carmen	71
Mirador Terraza San Pedro	65
Monkey Park	40
Monumento de los Caidos	51
Museo de Artesania Iberoamericana	64
Museo de Cerámica	65
Museo Municipal de Bellas Artes	52

N

Nightclubs	82
Nuestra Señora de la Concepción	52,71

O

Oasis del Valle	47
Orotava Valley	62

P

Paradores	73
Parque Ecologico las Aguilas del Teide	40